*God
of
Weakness*

God
of
Weakness

*How God Works Through
the Weak Things
of the World*

JOHN TIMMER

Zondervan Books
Zondervan Publishing House
Grand Rapids, Michigan

GOD OF WEAKNESS
Copyright © 1988 by John Timmer

Zondervan Books
are published by Zondervan Publishing House
1415 Lake Drive, S.E.
Grand Rapids, MI 49506

Library of Congress Cataloging in Publication Data

Timmer, John, 1927– .
  God of weakness.

  1. God. I. Title.
BT102.T55   1988   231.7   87-34063
ISBN 0-310-39421-X

Unless otherwise noted, all Scripture references are taken from the
Holy Bible: New International Version (North American Edition), copyright © 1973, 1978, 1984 by the International Bible Society. Used by
permission of Zondervan Bible Publishers.

The author and publisher would like to express their appreciation to
Pantheon Books, a division of Random House, for their kind permis-
sion in allowing us to reprint the statistical chart of Holocaust victims
on pages 82–83 of the present volume. It is reprinted from Albert
Friedlander's *Out of the Whirlwind*, originally published by Schocken
Books. We would also like to acknowledge Alfred A. Knopf, Inc., for
their permission in allowing us to quote the first stanza of John
Updike's poem "Seven Stanzas at Easter" from his collection *Telephone
Poles and Other Poems*, published in 1963 by Alfred A. Knopf, Inc.

Printed in the United States of America

88 89 90 91 92 93 / CH / 10 9 8 7 6 5 4 3 2

To my wife
Hazel

Contents

Foreword

I think my foundations would not shake much if God turned out to be four-in-one, or maybe two-in-one, instead of three-in-one, the way we believe he is, even though three-in-one has a lot to be said for it. But I would be devastated if John Timmer, at the end, where we all will know the truth, were to be proven wrong about God being the God of weakness.

Maybe I feel this way about Timmer's insight into God because I feel very weak and want with all my heart for God to be on my side. And because I see and feel so much weakness in other people, so much pain, so much craziness, so much poorness. God has to be on our side, and he has to make sense as the God who works inside, feels inside, suffers inside, and finally triumphs in and under and through weakness. He has to, I say, because otherwise he isn't the God of the Bible and isn't the God we need. If he isn't who John Timmer says he is, then he isn't a God who speaks to our condition.

And yet—oh, those upsetting words—and yet, there is something in me that does not want God *permanently* to be like John Timmer's God. Something in me wants him to be the God of weakness only until—and it ought to be soon—he has turned everything around. When my strength is renewed like eagles, when the poor become rich, the weak become powerful, then I want God to be the God of the rich and famous and powerful folk. But the truth must be that if the oppressed got to be in the driver's seat tomorrow, if the poor got to be rich and the rich became poor, if the hungry were fed and the satiated were sent away hungry, God would switch sides. He would be on the side of the nouveaux poor. For God *is* the God of weakness.

What makes John Timmer's insights so true and powerful for me is that he begins at the bottom, where life in its weakness and pain is lived, and lets us see God in his strange strength amid our weakness. In this book, God becomes transparent in the reality of our weakness.

Timmer has the good sense to know that nobody sees life's reality, the reality of our weakness, the way the artist—the novelist, for instance, or the poet—does. So he summons novelists, one after the other, each one saying just the right thing for Timmer's point of view, and lets them speak to us of life in concrete and living images, so that he, as the clear-headed theologian he is, can illumine God's relationship to that life, to that real life, in the sharp and vivid form of real people who tremble in their weakness the way a falling leaf flutters in the wind.

Theologians talk these days about beginning our theology down here, below heaven, down here on earth where we have to look at what is actually going on in order to talk truthfully about God up there. Timmer does not do this, exactly. But what he does do is better: he lets the God of heaven and earth, the God of creation and redemption, the God of the Bible, be seen for what he really is, the God of the struggler, the God of the defeated, the God of the poor, the God of the crazy, the God of the dying, and not the God of those who have it made in every way.

And he does it more honestly, more beautifully, more powerfully, more truly than anyone else on the evangelical scene today.

Lewis B. Smedes
Sierra Madre, 1987

Introduction

The title of this book is not *The Weakness of God*. It is, rather, *God of Weakness*. For God is not weak; he is all-powerful. Which immediately raises such questions as: If God is all-powerful, why do we see so little of that power? If God holds all the power, why doesn't he assert it? Why doesn't he make unhappy people happy, poor people rich, and sick people healthy? Why does he allow the poor to be exploited and the innocent to suffer? If God is all-powerful, why does he appear so weak?

The chapters that follow are responses to these and similar questions. This book explores what Swiss theologian Karl Barth once called the strange new world within the Bible. Barth experienced that when he brought human categories to this strange new world they proved to be of little help. He discovered that he had to start from the other end, that instead of looking at the Bible through his categories he had to look at his world through the Bible's categories.

This book, in a modest way, seeks to do something similar. As well-fed, well-dressed, well-housed, and well-insured Westerners, we unknowingly view the Bible through the glasses of our power and screen out the parts that threaten us. For these tell us that the basic viewpoint of the biblical writers is that of weakness. They tell us that God speaks where least expected to be heard and that he displays his power where least likely to be seen. They tell us that God's power is at work in our weakness and our dying rather than in our strength and our living.

In short, this book focuses on the unexpected, the illogical, and the unpredictable in God's behavior. It seeks to show, from a variety of angles, how God frequently brushes aside what is normative in our society, ignores what human convention expects of him, and defies roles that religious tradition ascribes to him.

God has a distinct dislike for human power. His preference clearly flows the other way. In bringing healing and salvation to our human race, he brings down the high and mighty and lifts up the weak and lowly.

1

GOD FROM THE EAST

To read the Bible is to travel from West to East. We are Western. The Bible is Eastern. When we open the Bible we find ourselves in a world where people think differently than we do, and thinking differently is precisely what we must do if we are to grow in our knowledge of a God who is strong but often appears weak.

God's power is a sovereign power, which means that he never allows us to command it. It also means that he exercises it in ways that are unpredictable and that he frequently brushes aside what to us is sacred and inviolable. God prefers our weakness to our strength, and he makes perfect his power in our weakness. "He has put down the mighty from their thrones," Luke reminds us, "and exalted those of low degree" (1:52 RSV).

To better understand how God exercises his power, we must reflect on what it means to be a Westerner reading an Eastern Bible. We must come to grips with the subtle matter of cultural interference.

None of us reads the Scriptures directly, for a filter called culture always separates us, to some extent, from the Bible. The light that flows from the Scriptures reaches us indirectly, shaped and colored by our culture with all its indigenous categories and values. And this filter can even screen out some of the light.

Western readers of the Bible fit Daniel J. Boorstin's description of American tourists:

We are probably the most traveled people of our time, or of any time. What is remarkable, on reflection, is not that our foreign travel has increased so much, but rather that all this travel has made so little difference in our thinking and feeling. Our travels have not, it seems, made us noticeably more cosmopolitan or more understanding of other peoples. The explanation is not that Americans are any more obtuse or uneducable than they used to be. Rather, the travel experience itself has been transformed.

In the past, travel abroad was expensive, dangerous, and difficult. Few could afford it. There were risks of disease and robbers, and comfortable accommodations were hard to find and equally hard to reach. But no longer. Travel agents have removed most of the hardship and danger from foreign travel—but at the great cost of insulating tourists from the people whose country they visit. Travel agencies offer us preplanned tours that make direct negotiation with native people unnecessary and that provide the same comforts—beds, meals, air conditioning, central heating, cars—that we enjoy at home.

Because of who we are (people who think in Western ways), we are similarly insulated from the people in the Bible. We lack a feel for the ethos of the Bible, and its mental landscape is as different from ours as its physical landscape is different from the Midwest. Both in origin and climate of thought the Bible is wholly Eastern. It is about Eastern people and Eastern customs, about Eastern morals and manners that are not readily accessible to us.

As a necessary first step, therefore, we must cultivate a greater sensitivity toward these East-West differences. We must venture to read the Scriptures with Eastern eyes. Since God's Word became flesh in an Eastern culture, we must minimize Western interference if we want to hear that Word in its original context. We must become familiar with the mental categories of the biblical writers themselves.

Just how does the East differ from the West? For that matter, what is the East? After all, Indonesia is as different from Japan, and Korea from India, as Sweden is from Italy or France from the United States. Like the West, the East has neither a unified system of thought nor a common pattern of behavior.

What do Easterners have in common? That question is not easy, for not everything we call Eastern can be found in every Eastern country, just as not everything we call Western can be found in all Western countries. And all of what we call Eastern is not absent from the West either. Nevertheless, there are some features that make up a distinctly Eastern ethos. "The great complex of Oriental nations," Martin Buber wrote, "can be shown to be one entity, an organism whose members, no matter how functionally different, have a similar structure and a similar vitality; and, as such, the Orient holds a position in its own right vis-à-vis the Occident." Hard though it may be to reduce this structure to words, we become most aware of it when we contrast East and West—as long as we remember that these contrasts are simplifications of matters that in reality are far more complex.

Outer Versus Inner

One major difference between West and East is that Westerners are more given to action, while Easterners are more given to contemplation. In our efforts to change the world, we Westerners are more apt to join crusades, leaving our own persons uncultivated, whereas Easterners put more trust in introspection.

I had my first intensive encounter with an Eastern contemplative discipline in September of 1973 when, along with some hundred others, I was the guest of the Saijoji Zen-temple in Odawara, Japan. At that time I had a keen interest in Japanese Buddhism and was especially interested in learning more about the technique of *Zazen* or "sitting in meditation."

Our first full day began at four-thirty in the morning. We were led through the darkness of the temple grounds to the large meditation hall where the resident Zen master taught us the first lessons in *Zazen*: how to sit cross-legged with straightened backbone, how to breathe, how to empty our minds of all acquisitive and competitive thoughts. We were told that contemplation is the key to wise action, that knowledge of self and understanding of life come only through disciplined exploring of that which is within us, and that without an inner agenda our outer agenda is like a tree without roots.

If it were possible to divorce the *Zazen* technique from its Buddhist rootage, it might be of great benefit to us Westerners with jittery minds and hyperactive bodies. Meditation, Buddhists believe, yields as many as twenty-eight benefits. It increases our vitality, helps us to recover from sickness, strengthens our will, makes us more efficient at our job, reduces the number of accidents we have, improves our thought processes, dispels our fears, and gives us self-confidence. Scientific research confirms many of these claims and suggests that meditation may even be of value in alleviating such typically Western diseases as alcoholism and drug addiction. It would yield immense economic benefits, for according to current estimates between five and thirteen percent of the U.S. work force abuses drugs other than alcohol. Numerous studies have shown, according to *Time* magazine, "that such abuse means up to three times as many job-related accidents and ten or more times as many sick days."

My praise of Zen meditation is not unqualified, however. *Zazen* is not a technique that can be transplanted easily from Buddhist into Christian soil, for its roots go deep into Buddhist metaphysics. The point is that the East, as exemplified by Zen, does a much better job than the West at lining up life's priorities. When it comes to the art of living, we action-oriented Westerners have much to learn from the East. The East, for many centuries, has lived by the conviction that a major portion of our energy should be expended on learning how to know and master the deep abyss from where our actions emanate.

If we Christians wish to know God better, we must learn to disengage ourselves from time to time from the whirl of activities that make us lose sight of the things that really give meaning to our life. We must learn to discern who we are and why we are. We must learn to decelerate our pace so that we may more nearly move in step with God. And the beginning of wisdom here is to create greater receptivity to God through the discipline of contemplation. Which is but another way of saying that before we are able to experience God's power and be propelled by it, we must first come to a discovery and confession of our weakness, a weakness that constantly keeps hiding behind our pursuit of self-worth and our drive to achieve and succeed.

One of the greatest pilots of our century was Sir Francis Chichester. In his small, single-engine plane, he hoped to be the first to fly nonstop across the Atlantic Ocean—but Lindbergh beat him to it. So he looked around for another barrier to break. He decided to fly the Tasman Sea, between Australia and New Zealand. This was in 1931 when navigation instruments were still rather primitive. All Chichester had was a compass and some basic instruments by which to determine his points of latitude and longitude. In planning his flight, Chichester chose the small island of Norfolk in the middle of the Tasman Sea—some nine hundred miles northeast of Sidney—as the place to refuel. He simply had to find this one-mile wide island. Either that or he would end up in the Tasman Sea.

After Chichester had been airborne for about an hour, the sky above him became overcast, which meant that he could no longer take his sightings on the sun and keep himself on course. How would he find that tiny island under a cloudy sky?

This was Chichester's solution. Whenever he saw a

break in the clouds, with the sunlight streaming through, he abandoned the course he was on, steered toward the sunlight, took out his compass and sextant, took his sighting on the sun, determined the correct course, and took off again under the clouds. He did this a couple of times and eventually found the island.

Chichester's experience is a parable of Christian living at its best. Before we begin our daily round of activities, we must first take our sightings. Either that or we will drift off course and end up drowning. To arrive at our destination, we must periodically move under the patch of God's sunlight and take our sightings for needed mid-course corrections.

As one wise man of the East put it: Life is like shooting an arrow. Before an arrow can be shot it must first be drawn back. If it is not drawn back on the string, it will fall limply from the hand of the archer. The same holds true for Christians. Unless we first withdraw in meditation the power of God will not propel us.

Having Versus Being

A second difference between West and East is that whereas Westerners are more concerned with having, Easterners are more concerned with being. Westerners are acquisitive. They seem to be out to gain control of the world. They see their needs and interests as the ultimate standard of right and wrong. When this is our outlook, the world turns into something to be exploited, something to satisfy our needs; the world around us then turns into a source of power, human life into a gold rush, and human beings into consumers.

But having many possessions inevitably interferes with our ability to be. The tables are turned on us and our possessions begin to possess us. We need burglar alarms and guns and insurance policies. Our house turns into a fortress—or a prison. The world outside appears increasingly hostile. Friendly people become suspect. Why are they so friendly? we wonder. What is it that they want?

There is a moving passage in Viktor Frankl's well-known book *Man's Search for Meaning.* In it, Frankl expresses how he felt when he reentered the world after having spent years inside the narrow confines of a Nazi concentration camp.

> I walked through the country past flowering meadows, for miles and miles, toward the market town near the camp. Larks rose to the sky and I could hear their joyous song. There was no one to be seen for miles around; there was nothing but the wide earth and sky and the lark's jubilation and the freedom of space. I stopped, looked around, and up to the sky—and then I went down on my knees. At that moment there was very little I knew of myself or of the world— I had but one sentence in mind—always the same: "I called to the Lord from my narrow prison and He answered me in the freedom of space."

When possessions possess us, we too are living in a narrow prison. Our luxuries and comforts block our vision. They wall us in and keep us from seeing the things that really matter. They don't allow us to see the flowers of the field and the birds of the air, nor the God who feeds and clothes them. When we are surrounded by automatic dryers and air conditioners and microwave ovens and home computers and videotape recorders and snowblowers and cottages and cars and recreational vehicles, it is difficult to concentrate on who and why we are. In one way or another these possessions keep us from focusing on the essentials.

More than once Jesus talked about the problem of seeing from inside our narrow prison. "The eye," he once said, "is the lamp of the body. If your eyes are good, your whole body will be full of light" (Matthew 6:22).

The Greek word for "good" here is *haplous.* And

haplous, literally, means folded but once. Now whatever is folded but once is simple. With each additional folding, matters become more complicated, as everyone knows who has tried to fold a piece of origami into a hippopotamus.

Jesus wants us to have eyes that are *haplous*, folded but once, simple. He wants us to focus on but one goal, to look in but one direction, to serve but one master and not two, not God and mammon, not God and possessions. An eye that is not "good" is an eye without a single focus, an eye that tries to focus on God and on our possessions simultaneously. The result is that both appear blurred.

Discerning the God of Scriptures requires a simple eye, a single attachment. And here the East has an advantage, for its best traditions seek detachment from the world of the senses and teach that craving is the root of all suffering.

Such a position places Easterners in an advantageous position in regards to God. For the God of Scripture is a God who pronounces the poor blessed. The poor are people who are not self-made and not self-sufficient. Because they are less walled in by what they possess, they are potentially more open to God. The reason Jesus warns the rich is not that he regards riches as bad per se, but rather that material prosperity easily isolates us from God. Riches of any kind represent power, and power gives us an advantage over others. It makes us independent from them. It also makes us feel independent from God. Jesus calls the poor blessed because the poor are able to listen to someone besides themselves, because they know they'll never manage on their own.

Poverty before God makes us more receptive to God's riches. Weakness before God makes us more receptive to his power.

I Versus We

A third difference between East and West surfaces in the way in which each views the individual and the community. Easterners tend to look at everything from the perspective of community; Westerners from that of the individual. Easterners extol communalism, Westerners individualism.

What is individualism? Kierkegaard answers this question in story form. Once, so his story goes, there was a farmer who went to the capital city to sell firewood. He sold so much and made so much money that he could afford to buy a new pair of shoes and a pair of stockings, and after these purchases he had enough money left over to get drunk. On his way home he fell asleep in the middle of the highway. After a while a wagon came along. Not wishing to get down from his wagon, the driver shouted, "Hey you! Either get up or I'll drive over your legs!" The farmer, still drunk, looked at his legs and because he did not recognize them as his by reason of the shoes and stockings, cried out, "Go ahead! They aren't my legs!"

Individualism asks, "Am I my brother's legs' keeper?" This kind of individualism is as alien to the spirit of the Scriptures as love of possessions is. Individualism is destructive of true community and therefore works against the Holy Spirit who seeks to incorporate people into the body of Christ.

Individualism also influences the way we view non-Christians. It sees them as objects to be saved, not as human beings. It attaches great importance to numbers and statistics. It uses such terms as "the business of witnessing" and "cost per person." In the selection of a mission field it makes us choose one field over another because it appears more cost-effective, meaning that it promises to yield a larger number of converts for the same amount of money.

Easterners look at people differently. They view them as members of a community, as representatives of a totality. So does the Bible. It is not impressed by numbers. It thinks in terms of "firstfruits," which means that it sees the future of a people or of a nation as contained in the first converts. Paul, for example, calls the household of Stephanas the "firstfruits of Achaia" (1 Corinthians 16:15 KJV). He looks at this handful of people as representatives of all the people in Achaia.

We Westerners are such rabid individualists that the idea of firstfruits never occurs to us. We are enthralled or disappointed by numbers and statistics. The Bible never is. It sees the many contained in the few. It sees the "I" contained in the "We." It is not discouraged by small numbers. It sees the power of God at work in the firstfruits, not many of whom are wise or powerful or of noble birth.

Future Versus Past

A fourth difference between West and East is that Westerners tend to derive their direction from the future, while Easterners tend to do so from the past.

For example, we invest heavily in future projections: how many babies are going to be born in the next ten years, how many couples will seek a divorce, what the average life span is going to be twenty years from now, what the outcome of the next election will be. We seek to gain this information so that when the future arrives it will hold few surprises for us.

Easterners think differently. To them the past, rather than the future, is directive. To them the past is not dead but alive and still active. This, of course, is a part of their strong sense of community, the community that includes not just the living but the dead as well. To forget the past is to sin against the community; to remember the past is to honor and sustain it.

When I was a young missionary to Japan in the early sixties, this was one of the first things I learned about the East. On my evening strolls through our neighborhood I observed how certain people engaged in ancestral worship every day. *Why every day?* I wondered. The answer, it dawned on me, lies in their strong sense of community of which the spirits of departed ancestors continue to be a vital part. To secure their blessing, these spirits must be honored and appeased regularly.

The past is not dead; it lives on in the community. This is true also of the biblical past. It lives on in the community that remembers this past. Abraham and Isaac and Jacob are living members of the community of faith, which is why God calls himself " 'the God of Abraham, the God of Isaac, and the God of Jacob.' He is not the God of the dead, but of the living" (Mark 12:26–27).

When it comes to relating to the past, we Americans work under a special handicap: We have poor memories. Millions of immigrants who came to our shores wished to forget their pasts. They tried to get away from what they didn't like or didn't want, and their escape from the past, somehow, has gotten into our blood.

As American Christians, therefore, we work under a severe handicap in trying to understand the God of the Scriptures. For God speaks to us, not directly, not through visions or dreams or mystical experiences, but through the remembered past. What to us appears weak or dead—the past—to God is a channel through which his power reaches us.

Westerners, more than Easterners, are activistic, acquisitive, self-centered, and future-oriented, although none of these characteristics, of course, is absent from the people of the East. The Easterner's cultural climate, however, places a much higher premium on the contemplative, personal awareness, the community, and the past. And it was through such a culture that God chose to reveal himself to us.

As Westerners, we tend to interpret the Scriptures in terms of our own cultural categories, forgetting that other cultures have categories that, though different, may be just as valid. So we have done and continue to do. And we do so unconsciously.

An illustration: In 1966 the Christian novelist Shusaku Endo published his novel *Silence*. It became an immediate best-seller. Later it was made into a movie, which, in 1971, won the grand prize at a prominent arts festival.

Endo's purpose was to contrast Eastern and Western ways of looking at Christianity. Japanese people, he says, "have warded off Christianity as a harsh, severe, judgmental, paternal religion. . . . In *Silence* I stressed the maternal side of Christianity." The Japanese, he is saying, need to reconcile Western Christianity with their indigenous Eastern experience.

Endo's plot is based on a true story—the apostasy of the seventeenth century Portuguese Jesuit Ferreira, the Superior of the Jesuits in Japan who had been active there as a missionary for twenty years.

Endo's story leads up to an encounter between Ferreira and Rodrigues, who is also a Jesuit and a former student of his. Rodrigues has traveled all the way to Japan for the specific purpose of finding out what has happened to his former teacher. Soon after his arrival he is arrested by the Japanese authorities and through them brought in contact with Ferreira. As these two men meet again after so many years the following conversation develops.

FERREIRA: For twenty years I have labored in this country. I know it better than you.

RODRIGUES: During those twenty years as Superior you did marvelous work. I read with great respect the letters you sent to the headquarters of the Society.

FERREIRA: Well, before your eyes stands the figure of an old missionary defeated by missionary work.

RODRIGUES: No one can be defeated by missionary work. When you and I are dead yet another missionary will board a

	junk at Macao and secretly come ashore somewhere in this country.
FERREIRA:	For twenty years I labored in the mission. The one thing I know is that our religion does not take root in this country.
RODRIGUES:	It is not that it does not take root. It's that the roots are torn up.
FERREIRA:	This country is a swamp. In time you will come to see that for yourself. This country is a more terrible swamp than you can imagine. Whenever you plant a sapling in this swamp the roots begin to rot; the leaves grow yellow and wither. And we have planted the sapling of Christianity in this swamp.

After this conversation, Rodrigues passes through a crisis of faith. To understand the nature of this crisis it is important to know that after the Japanese government officially proscribed Christianity it applied the so-called *fumie* test to those suspected of being Christians. The word *fumi* means to step; the word *e* means picture. A *fumie* was a copper or bronze image of Jesus mounted on a piece of wood on which people suspected of being Christian were asked to step. Anyone stepping on it either was not a Christian or was a Christian who, in the eyes of the Japanese government, had now become an apostate.

After his conversation with Ferreira, Rodrigues is given the choice of dying a martyr's death or stepping on the *fumie*, thereby saving not only his own life but also the lives of several Christians presently hanging upside down over a cesspool.

In this decision Rodrigues does not simply act as an individual but as a representative of the persecuted Christians. And this communal responsibility makes him decide to make the dreaded step. This is how Endo tells it:

The priest raises his foot. In it he feels a dull, heavy pain. This is no mere formality. He will now trample on what he has considered the most beautiful thing in his life, on what he has believed most pure, on what is filled with the ideals and the dreams of man. How his foot aches! And then the Christ in bronze speaks to the priest: "Trample! Trample! I more than anyone know of the pain in your foot. Trample! It was to be trampled on by men that I was born into this world. It was to share men's pain that I carried my cross." The priest placed his foot on the *fumie*. Dawn broke. And far in the distance the cock crew.

In *Silence*, Endo pictures the clash between the Western and the Japanese perception of the Christian faith. The Western perception as brought to Japan by the early Catholic missionaries was that of God as a stern father who, when his children misbehave, becomes angry and punishes. The Japanese perception was that of God as a mother who understands the failures of her children and takes them under her protection.

God, Endo is saying, is a God of maternal love. And such love is frequently powerless and invisible, so that we might conclude that God does not exist or that he is silent or perhaps angry. The God as preached, first by Ferreira and then by Rodrigues, is a God resembling an authoritarian father. What both men must learn is that he is more like a mother who shares the suffering and failures of her children and weeps with them.

When the gospel first came to Japan in the sixteenth century, many people flocked to it and were baptized. But no sooner was Christianity proscribed than many of them stepped on the *fumie*. Still, this did not mean the end of their Christian confession. On the contrary, says Endo, through this external denial they came to experience the love of Christ in a new and unexpected way. Such is the experience of the Portuguese Jesuit Rodrigues, of whom

Endo writes in the final paragraph of *Silence*: "No doubt his fellow priests would condemn his act as sacrilege; but even if he was betraying them, he was not betraying his Lord. He loved him now in a different way from before. Everything that had taken place until now had been necessary to bring him to this love."

Eastern rejection of Western forms of Christianity may not be due so much to the built-in offense of the gospel as to our own Western way of reading the Scriptures. We always read them, darkly, through our culture's categories so that some aspects are accentuated and others obscured. Endo challenges us to read them through different eyes—through Eastern eyes.

2

GOD OF WEAK PARTNERS

In Graham Greene's novel *The Power and the Glory*, God's power and glory burst forth in a most unlikely candidate—a Roman Catholic priest who is hooked on alcohol and fathers an illegitimate child with one of his parishioners. This priest is at once a pathetic and a hopeful figure.

The setting of the story is Mexico in the thirties, during a time when the government is persecuting the church. The church is again what it was in the early centuries—a church of the catacombs. It meets in mud huts; the altar is made of packing cases; the communion chalice is a chipped cup; the wafer a dry crust of bread. Stripped of temporal power, the Mexican church experiences the power of a growing dependence on God. In the state of Tabasco, where the story takes place, priests are allowed to stay only if they marry.

The priest of the story is a coward. He is on the run and there is a reward on his head. Pursued by a police lieutenant through the swamps and forests of Tabasco, he slips into villages, says mass, baptizes children, and hears hastily recited confessions. He is a weakling and he knows it. The source of his courage to continue in the face of such odds is not so much his faith as it is an occasional bottle of brandy.

Then things go from bad to worse. First he gives up on the prescribed days of abstinence. Then he quits reading the breviary regularly. Then he ceases to celebrate

Mass on a stone altar, as prescribed; the dumb thing is too heavy and slows him down. And finally there are moral failures: fornication and constant drinking.

Still, derelict and degenerate though he is, he remains God's chosen instrument of grace. He is not the kind that says, "Let us sin that grace may abound." Rather, he is ashamed of his weakness but at the same time amazed that God uses his ministry in spite of it. "Don't look at me," he seems to be saying to those around him, "look at God. If God loves me, he certainly loves you too!"

Gradually he is stripped of all pride and develops a genuine humility. Caught at last and put in prison, he awaits his final hour. As he sits in his cell, he thinks: "I have been drunk—I don't know how many times; there isn't a duty I haven't neglected; I have been guilty of pride, lack of charity. . . . If I hadn't been so useless, useless . . . If I had only one soul to offer, so that I could say: Look what I've done." Tears pour down his face, because he must go to God with nothing to show for his life but his own weakness.

Nevertheless, this weakling, chosen by God to be his witness in life and his martyr in death, is a prime example of what Paul writes in 2 Corinthians 4:7: "We have this treasure in jars of clay to show that this all-surpassing power is from God and not from us." That treasure is the power and glory of God's grace, and the jars of clay in which it is contained are the people God chooses to display it.

The first people that God chose in this way were, of course, the people of Israel. As God's partners, they were at least as unlikely as Graham Greene's fornicating whiskey-priest.

Israel: God's Unlikely Partner

As we read Scripture, we might well ask: Why did God choose Israel as his partner? Why didn't he, instead, choose Egypt? Egypt, after all, had the strongest army and the greatest wealth in the world. Its power in the world was unrivaled. Pharaoh was in a position to force Yahweh on every nation within reach. He could have issued a royal decree to this effect in every province and satellite nation, and he could have dispatched his armies to the unconquered lands on a holy mission. Or centuries later, God could have used the Babylonians at their peak of world power. Or still later, the Greeks with their philosophy and science. Or the Romans with their genius for law and order. Or the Americans with their uncanny ability to make things work and get things done.

It would seem that with any of these choices God's mission in the world would have fared much better. Why then, to bless the people of the world, did God want to work through a people who, when he called them, were not even a people but just a crew of slaves?

From God's perspective, though, such a choice had definite advantages. It allowed him to mold Israel like a lump of unformed clay and shape it into the kind of people that would not be constantly looking back over its shoulders to its "glorious past" and its "hallowed traditions." God first creates whom he chooses. That way the chosen people won't boast and think that God chose them because of what they have to offer. To bless the world, God chose as his partner a people of little strength and no repute.

How, in the dog-eat-dog world of power politics, was this people to survive? How do small and weak nations survive today? By entering into military alliances with strong nations. By moving under the protective umbrella of nations with powerful armies. It was no different for Israel. To survive, it had to enter into an alliance with a party strong enough to ward off attacks by powerful nations. God offered to be that party. He entered into a covenant with Israel, and under the protection of this covenant Israel can live and travel in safety.

Accordingly, when Pharaoh pursued the Israelites

with "six hundred of the best chariots, along with all the other chariots of Egypt," Moses told his people, "Do not be afraid. Stand firm and you will see the deliverance the Lord will bring you today. . . . The Lord will fight for you; you need only to be still" (Exodus 14:7, 13, 14). For that is what a covenant partner is for, to protect the weak partner from predators.

Israel need not be strong, *should not* be strong if it is to bear witness to the power of God's liberating grace. All it must do is have faith in its partner.

It is as though Israel lived in two worlds—the world of sight and the world of faith. The world of sight is the world of the survival of the fittest. The world of faith is the world of God's hidden rule where the weak are cherished and slaves are royalty. This hidden world is invisible and only rarely breaks in upon our vision. It is like the world the policeman represents in Kafka's parable "Give it Up":

> It was very early in the morning, the streets clean and deserted, I was on my way to the station. As I compared the tower clock with my watch I realized it was much later than I had thought and that I had to hurry; the shock of this discovery made me feel uncertain of the way, I wasn't very well acquainted with the town as yet; fortunately, there was a policeman at hand, I ran to him and breathlessly asked him the way. He smiled and said: "You asking me the way?" "Yes," I said, "since I can't find it myself." "Give it up! Give it up!" said he, and turned with a sudden jerk, like someone who wants to be alone with his laughter.

The outcome of the story shocks us. It is absurd. It violates normal social behavior. As the person is hurrying to the station, becomes disoriented, and then turns to a nearby policeman, the reader feels confident that the policeman will end the uncertainty. For if a policeman doesn't know the way around town, who does? He is the final authority. The policeman's answer, "Give it up!" cracks the realism of the story. And through the crack we catch a glimpse of a different world—a world ruled by different values, a world in which people's behavior answers to different norms.

Kafka's story helps us understand the oddness of things in God's world, how topsy-turvy they are. The story of God choosing Israel as his partner is not what we would ordinarily call a "real life" story. For in "real life" slaves don't usually escape subjugation and seas don't open to offer passage to the weak and swallow up the strong.

God's choice of Israel makes us aware of the reality of these two worlds. One is the world *we* want to live in and the other is the world *God* wants us to live in. It's a story that enables us to see through the veil of everydayness and catch a glimpse of a world where our expectations are turned on their heads. Israel's constant temptation (and their tragedy) was that it sought to live in the same world as all the other nations. But the more it does, the farther it moves from under the protection that living in God's world offers. God wants Israel to live in an upside-down world where none of our common-sense rules work. But Israel can't believe that God really wants it to be different, anymore than we can believe, for instance, that God wants us to turn the other cheek and love our enemy.

Listen, America?

To understand Israel as God's partner we must see it as a fragile jar of clay that contains the treasure of God's saving grace.

In his famous ninety-five theses posted on the door of the Wittenberg Castle Church, Martin Luther addressed this anomaly. His key thesis, number sixty-two, reads, "The true treasure of the church is the most holy gospel of the glory and grace of God." This is followed by thesis sixty-three, "But this treasure is naturally most odious, for it makes the first to be the last." Entrusting the treasure of God's grace to jars of clay is offensive, Luther is saying, because it turns all human values upside down. God puts his treasure into these jars, not because nothing better is available, but because God chooses to accomplish his saving purpose through the medium of human weakness rather than of strength.

Christoph Blumhardt, a famous nineteenth-century German preacher, once said, "The Savior doesn't need strong people. . . . He needs beaten people who are afraid they will be disobedient to his commands, people who tremble and falter and stand in awe before the word of truth."

Always it is upon human weakness, not upon human strength, that God chooses to build his kingdom. Nothing can defeat a believer who says, "Lord, here is my weakness. I dedicate it to you." This is the victory that overcomes the world. To understand Israel's role in history we must constantly force ourselves to view it as a jar of clay that contains the treasure of God's saving power.

This is the problem with some current Christian views of Israel. The temptation is to see Israel from the perspective of power. For example, in his book *Listen, America!* Jerry Falwell urges American Christians to stand with the Israeli Jews. "Every nation that has ever stood with the Jews has felt the hand of God's blessing on them. I firmly believe God has blessed America because America has blessed the Jews. If this nation wants her fields to remain white with grain, her scientific achievements to remain notable, and her freedom to remain intact, America must continue to stand with Israel."

Why? Because modern Israel, it is argued, is the fulfillment of Old Testament prophecies. While dispersed among the nations, the Jews tenaciously clung to the prophetic promises that one day they would return to their homeland, there to prosper. On May 14, 1948, with the establishment of Israel as a nation, and with Israel's survival of the wars waged against her since that day, these prophecies have been fulfilled, according to Falwell.

Though God may well be finished with the nations that seek to destroy Israel, God is not yet finished with the nation of Israel. His promise to modern Israel is: "I will bless those who bless you, and whoever curses you I will curse" (Genesis 12:3). Therefore, reasons Falwell, America, in its foreign policy, must always stand with the Israelis. Solidarity with Israel yields divine dividends. America must never yield to Arab pressure and trade her allegiance with Israel for allegiance to the oil-producing Arab nations. To do so would be trading "her position of world leadership for a place in the history books alongside of Rome. We cannot allow that to happen."

But Falwell misunderstands Israel's history and the nature of God's topsy-turvy world revealed through it. Falwell seems to be more interested in power than in weakness, more in success than in failure. But Israel's history testifies to God's predilection for human weakness as his main avenue of blessing. And this God who chose slaves to be his partners, when he fully entered the life of humanity, chose a stable and a manger by which to make his entrée. He became human at the lowest position that people in their hunger for power allow him to have.

And Jesus always maintained that lowest position. Standing before King Herod, one of the power brokers of his age, Jesus exhibited total powerlessness. Speechless, he offered no defense. He said nothing and did nothing. He allowed himself to be moved around like a pawn in the power play of the high and mighty.

It was the sight of this powerless Jesus that Friedrich Nietzsche found so offensive. The only proper word for Jesus' attitude before worldly power, he said, is "idiot." After Nietzsche's death, his sister edited out this word; she found it too shocking. But Nietzsche meant what he wrote. It was his way of saying that Jesus defied all human categories of reason and sanity when he allowed himself to be pushed around.

Falwell's view is less insightful—but far more popular. It appeals to something that lives in all of us, for somehow we all venerate power and believe that it is by power that people prevail. And the next step is to think that if God is to prevail in history he will choose what is strong over what is weak.

Falwell identifies the Israel of the Bible with the modern state of Israel and therefore with a nation that relies on its great military strength to survive in the midst of heavily armed Arab hostility. But the Israel God chose as his partner was not the Israel of power. It was the Israel of weakness, the Israel that waits for God.

The 1980s: Countdown to Armageddon?

But Falwell is not alone. Hal Lindsey's views, in broad outline, are similar to Falwell's and are widely known through his book *The Late Great Planet Earth* and also through such later prophetic updates as *The 1980s: Countdown to Armageddon.*

Lindsey's books remind me of certain medieval writings, now called the Sibylline Oracles, that in their day were as popular as Lindsey's writings are in ours. These Oracles grew up alongside the Scriptures and became just as influential. Throughout the Middle Ages, Sibylline eschatology competed with biblical eschatology and had the temporary advantage over the latter in that it was adaptable and could constantly be updated to fit recent developments.

These Sibylline Oracles catered to the popular craving for unquestionable forecasts of future events. Writes Norman Cohn:

> People were always on the watch for the "signs" which, according to the prophetic tradition, were to herald and accompany the final "time of troubles"; and since the "signs" included bad rulers, civil discord, war, drought, famine, plague, comets, sudden deaths of promi-

nent persons, and an increase in general sin-fulness, there was never any difficulty about finding them. Invasion or the threat of invasion by Huns, Magyars, Mongols, Saracens or Turks always stirred memories of those hordes of Antichrist, the peoples of Gog and Magog.

Lindsey's is a Robert Ludlum look at power, a lot of action, suspense, and gratuitous violence, which sells books but only tenuously relates to the God whose power and glory shine brightly through Israel's weakness.

The Church: God's Compromising Partner

In his first letter to the Corinthians, Paul offers this description of the earliest church in Corinth: "Not many of you were wise by human standards; not many were influential; not many were of noble birth. But God chose the foolish things of the world to shame the wise; God chose the weak things of the world to shame the strong. He chose the lowly things of this world and the despised things—and the things that are not—to nullify the things that are, so that no one may boast before him" (1:26–29).

The church, in other words, answers to the same description as Israel. When God chose Israel, he did not first look over a number of nations and then choose Israel. When God elected Israel, Israel as a nation did not even exist. God first had to create it out of nothing. In the same way, when God first called the church into being he did not first look over a number of people and then make a selection. Rather, he created it. The church is a new creation. To survive, it must live by the same rules as Israel did.

Furthermore, the church has God's "treasure in jars of clay to show that this all-surpassing power is from God and not from us" (2 Corinthians 4:7). It must allow the brilliance of God's face to shine through its wrinkles and bald spots. Whenever Christians raise themselves above their intended status, whenever they seek to upgrade their material from clay to stainless steel, the conditions under which they exist slip away from them.

God can use a church best when it stops aiming at success and growth and influence. It is sad how many Christians, in such a success-oriented environment, say things like, "God can't use me; I'm not educated enough," or "I'm not spiritual enough," or "I am not moral enough"; it is sad because, in reality, it is through what we consider to be our disqualifying weaknesses that God's power is repeatedly and surprisingly revealed.

Religion of the Weak

Christianity, noted Simone Weil, is preeminently the religion of slaves. Slaves cannot help but belong to it. This was true of Paul's day, when many Christians in the Gentile churches were slaves, and it is also true in our day. By its very nature the Christian faith is the faith of the oppressed and the afflicted, of people at the bottom of everybody's list.

To drive this point home Jesus once told a story (Luke 14:16–24): "A certain man was preparing a great banquet and invited many guests." After counting the number of accepted invitations, things get under way and can no longer be stopped. Animals are killed that must be eaten that same day. Those who accepted the invitation must show up. To make sure they do, the host sends his servant to them with a second message, "Come, for everything is now ready." Meaning: the meat is cooked and we are ready to serve.

At this point in the story Jesus throws a curve ball at his audience. He violates the realism of the story and, in violating it, allows us to catch a glimpse of God's world.

All the people who had accepted the invitation now begin to make excuses. The first says, "I have just bought a field, and I must go and see it"—which is an outright lie, for in the East no one buys a field who has not previously checked out whether it has a well, whether it is walled in, whether there are paths cutting across it, whether there are trees on it, who the previous owner was, and what profit it yielded during the past few years. All these things are checked out before a field is bought. And now the host is to believe that the field has been bought sight unseen!

The other excuses are equally lame, so that when he hears them the host goes through the ceiling and immediately draws up a new guest list. "Go out quickly into the streets and alleys of the town and bring in the poor, the crippled, the blind and the lame"—all to whom the host is not indebted and who are not able to respond in kind, unlike those who were first invited.

These are the people for whom the church was created—for the marginal, the riffraff, the oppressed, the poor, for all who have nothing to offer God except their poverty. As long as the church was that kind of community, it was true to its nature and flourished. But no sooner did it ally itself with the powerful then the process of decay set in, for power corrupts even the most well intentioned.

After the Edict of Milan in A.D. 313, which ended the official Roman persecution of the Christians, and after the imperial edict of A.D. 380, which obligated all Roman citizens to become Christians, the Christian faith became mixed with faith in Roman civilization and the church measured its health partly by how well it succeeded in contributing to the stability of the empire.

Church worship began to be influenced by the ceremonies of the imperial court. Incense, used as a symbol of respect for the emperor, began appearing in churches. Bishops, who until then had worn everyday clothes, began dressing like Roman consuls. The church allied itself with the status quo and surrendered much of its prophetic mission and became the religious right arm of the state. This situation, with all sorts of local variations and exceptions, has lasted into our own century.

In his autobiography, former Prime Minister Nehru

of India observes how different Western countries have adopted different animals as expressions of national character and ambition. For example, Germany and the United States have adopted the eagle; Holland and Great Britain, the lion; and Russia, the bear. All of these are aggressive animals, animals of prey. It is not surprising, therefore, writes Nehru, that people growing up with these symbols develop aggressive attitudes. They look upon others as potential prey. Then Nehru asks this question: Why is it that the Hindu is so much gentler and abhors violence? Could it be because his animal of protection is the cow?

When I first read these words I was expecting him to ask: Why is it that the *Christian* is so much gentler? Christians, after all, have identified themselves with sheep. Nehru's commendation of the Hindu caught me off guard. It bothered me because it was an implicit indictment of much of Western Christianity, which has been anything but gentle.

At one point in his ministry, Jesus described the mission of his followers in these words, "I am sending you out like sheep among wolves" (Matthew 10:16). Because Western Christians throughout the many centuries of their history have so consistently looked at their own defenselessness rather than at the protective rod and staff of the Good Shepherd, they frequently lost sight of their mission as sheep among wolves and behaved like wolves instead, allying themselves with political power, financial wealth, and national purpose. The result is that they degraded Christianity into a civil religion.

From an unknown second- or third-century Greek Christian who defended the Christian faith like a sheep among wolves come these words:

> [Christians] are obedient to the appointed laws, but persecuted by all. They are not understood, and they are condemned. They are put to death, and they are made alive. They are poor, and they

make many rich. They lack all things, and they abound in everything. They are dishonored, and they are disglorified in their dishonor. They are evil spoken of, and they are justified. They are reviled, and they bless. They are insulted, and they give honor. While doing good, they are punished as evil. Being punished, they rejoice as being made alive. . . . God has appointed them to such a post which it is not lawful for them to desert.

Similar testimonies now reach us from behind the Iron Curtain. One of the most remarkable facts of contemporary church history is the revival of the Christian faith in Soviet Russia. Under the Czarist regime it was the ally of the status quo. Then came the Russian Revolution. Much within the Russian Orthodox Church went out with the political system to which it was tied. But now we hear repeated reports of a rebirth of the Christian faith in Russia—a country where Christianity is attacked with wolflike brutality. According to the latest, though perhaps exaggerated statistics, "every third adult Russian (Russians represent about half of all Soviet citizens) and every fifth adult Soviet human being is said to be a practicing Christian" (from Hans Küng's *On Being a Christian*).

What accounts for this spiritual rebirth? One answer, writes a Russian Christian (writing pseudonymously to avoid government harassment), is that "we have experienced such utter exhaustion of human resources that we have learned to see the 'one essential' that cannot be taken away from man, and we have learned not to look to human resources for succor. In glorious destitution, in utter defenselessness in the face of suffering, our hearts have been kindled by an inner spiritual warmth and have opened to new, unexpected impulses."

Why haven't many years of brainwashing and oppression by a hostile regime been able to destroy the church? Why has a flock of weak, defenseless sheep been able to survive for so long among the wolves? Because the Lord is the kind of shepherd who prepares a pasture ahead of his sheep by uprooting poisonous weeds, cutting off thistles, and uncovering nests of snakes and scorpions.

3

GOD OF DEAD ENDS

Few books offer a better introduction to the main theme of the Bible than Dostoyevski's novel *Crime and Punishment*.

The main characters are Raskolnikov and Sonia. Raskolnikov is a murderer. With the blunt side of an axe he has bludgeoned Alyona Ivanovna, an old pawnbroker, to death. His motive is his belief that there are two kinds of people—inferior people, who only exist to reproduce their kind, and people who have the gift to utter a "new word." In Raskolnikov's estimation, the old pawnbroker belongs to the first kind. She lived a parasitical life. But he classifies himself as belonging to the gifted people, and such people, for the sake of achieving a higher goal, may at times be forced "to step over a corpse or wade through blood" without having to feel any moral compunction. And, as Raskolnikov reasons, is not the destruction of Alyona Ivanovna, who lived the life of a louse, such a higher goal?

Sonia too does wrong for the sake of a higher goal. Because of her father's alcoholism, her stepmother and three stepsisters live in constant misery and poverty. To shield them against an even worse fate, Sonia becomes a prostitute, although, unlike Raskolnikov, Sonia does not seek to justify herself—nor does her father who harbors deep guilt feelings. He believes that Sonia will be forgiven for what his drinking drove her to. God will forgive her, he explains to Raskolnikov, because Sonia has sinned only for her family's sake. God will, says Sonia's father,

> come in that day and he will ask, "Where is the daughter who gave herself for her cross, consumptive stepmother and for the little children of another? Where is the daughter who had pity upon the filthy drunkard, her earthly father, undismayed by his beastliness?" And he will say, "Come to me! I have already forgiven thee once . . . I have forgiven thee once. . . . Thy sins which are many are forgiven thee for thou hast loved much . . ." And he will forgive my Sonia, he will forgive, I know it . . .

One day Raskolnikov asks Sonia, "Tell me how this shame and degradation can exist in you side by side with other, opposite, holy feelings? It would be better, a thousand times better and wiser to leap into the water and end it all!" Raskolnikov can see no high purpose in what Sonia is doing, only a dead end. The way he sees it, Sonia has but three options. She can jump into a canal and drown. She can go out of her mind. Or she can at last "sink into depravity which obscures the mind and turns the heart to stone."

After a while their conversation turns to the story of the resurrection of Lazarus. "Where is the story of Lazarus?" Raskolnikov asks.

"It's in the fourth Gospel," Sonia whispers.

"Find it and read it to me," he says.

Sonia opens the old and worn New Testament and finds the place. At first her hands are shaking and her voice fails. But then she reads: "Now a man was sick. He was from Bethany, the village of Mary and her sister Martha . . ." On and on she reads, and when she comes to the place where Jesus goes to Lazarus' grave and weeps, Sonia begins to tremble. She is getting near the account of the greatest miracle when Jesus cries with a loud voice, "Lazarus, come out!" A feeling of immense triumph comes over her and gives power to her voice. The lines dance before her eyes, but it does not matter— she knows it by heart.

As Sonia the streetwalker reads the story to Raskolnikov the murderer, she explains to him what it is to have reached a dead end, but also what it means to know him who can make all things new. She knows that she cannot lift herself out of the profession into which she has sunk under the pressure of family need. Her only hope is the miracle of resurrection. "What would I be," she asks, "without the God who raised up Lazarus, who in a wondrous miracle can also raise me from death to life?"

Dostoyevski's story leads to the heart of the Christian gospel, for the deepest and most pervasive theme of the New Testament is resurrection. The four Gospels are not biographical accounts of Jesus' life. Their single purpose, rather, is to proclaim the cheering news of his resurrection.

Nor do the Gospels receive their sharpest focus from the things Jesus taught, though it is a common mistake to think that they do. The Sermon on the Mount, Jesus' best-known message, is often held up as the essence of what Jesus has to offer to the world. This sermon, some people claim, presents Christlike life at its purest, so that, if it were to be written into the constitution and laws of the nations and enforced, it would usher in heaven on earth. To say this, however, is to say that even if Jesus had not been raised from the dead, there would still be a gospel able to stand on its own two feet and worthy of universal acceptance.

But the early Christians did not think there was such a gospel. To them the gospel without Jesus' resurrection was no gospel at all. Jesus, it is true, did great things and taught great truths, but so, after all, did men like Elijah and Nathan and John the Baptist, though to a lesser degree. Still, in their day, these had been truly great teachers. But all of them died. And with each new generation their influence faded, until at last it ceased to have much effect.

A similar thing would have happened if Jesus had not risen, which is why Jesus never allowed his disciples to rest in anything he said. He never let them rest, say, in the Sermon on the Mount, but always led them on to the mystery and paradox of his person. He repeatedly told them that if they wished to understand who he was, they should not look so much to the past as to the future when the purpose of his coming would be fully revealed. This left his disciples confused and mystified, in which state they would have remained had not Jesus been raised from the dead. Only then did the pieces of his life begin to fit into a meaningful pattern.

But what if Jesus had not been raised? What if, instead of a dominant mountain, Jesus' resurrection had been a crater? Measuring the magnitude of Jesus' resurrection against its absence, the apostle Paul is of the opinion that in that case all preaching and faith amounts to an exercise in futility. Then, he says, we are still stuck in our sin. Then those beautiful words chiseled on so many tombstones are all a big lie. Then life adds up to zero. And the church collapses.

John Updike puts it this way in the first of his "Seven Stanzas at Easter":

> Make no mistake: if He rose at all
> it was as His body;
> if the cells' dissolution did not reverse, the
>   molecules reknit,
> the amino acids rekindle,
> the Church will fall.

Updike's "either/or" faithfully reflects Paul's assessment of Jesus' resurrection. Either he did rise and life has meaning, or he didn't, in which case we are adrift in a void.

In Martin Gardner's novel *The Flight of Peter Fromm*, there is a scene in which Peter, the protagonist, enters the living room of his Chicago Divinity School mentor one late summer afternoon, a thick volume in his hand and an expression of deep distress on his face. The book is a single-volume edition of Reinhold Niebuhr's two greatest works: *Human Nature* and *Human Destiny.*

Before coming to Chicago, Peter was a Pentecostal and a dreamer of dreams. One of his dreams was to start a new Protestant Reformation. The hour of decision had come for America, he thought, and the fullness of time for a great revival to sweep the nation had arrived. And Peter Fromm believed that God had chosen him to lead this revival.

To make this dream come true, Peter conceived a bold plan. He would not enroll in a seminary that was theologically sound. Instead, he would enter the very citadel of the enemy. He would master all the modern learning that a great secular university had to offer. He would examine and expose every false argument. He would dissect the diseased heart of liberal theology nerve by nerve, artery by artery.

And so Peter Fromm had entered the most liberal of liberal seminaries: the University of Chicago Divinity School. But the more he exposed himself to modern learning, the more his Pentecostal faith began to crumble, until at last only one article of his original creed remained—that of Jesus' bodily resurrection. But this final article too eventually began to erode.

Tapping a finger on the cover of Niebuhr's book on that summer afternoon Peter says angrily, "Can you imagine this? There are six hundred pages here. It's a full statement of the theology of America's most famous Protestant thinker. How many references do you suppose there are to the Resurrection of Christ?"

"How many?" Dr. Wilson asks.

"Not one! Not a single one! Here, let me show you." And Peter picks up the book again and goes to the index. Under the heading, "Christ—divinity of," he points out, are many subheads. But none concerns the Resurrection.

Then he thumbs back a few pages. "And here," he says, "is an index of all the scriptural passages quoted or cited in the book. Not a single passage from Matthew twenty-eight, Mark sixteen, Luke twenty-four, and John twenty, the four Resurrection chapters!"

"And first Corinthians fifteen," Peter says. "Niebuhr does have a few quotes from *that* chapter, but they're not about the Resurrection."

"And so," Peter says, "it means that Reinie just won't tell us what he thinks. I've wasted two weeks trying to find out. I even asked a student who did work under him at Union. *He* didn't know either. Can you beat that? How can a man write six-hundred pages about Christian theology and not say what he believes about the biggest miracle in the Bible?"

How indeed? For if Christ has not been raised, the Christian's faith is useless. Christ's resurrection casts a light backward over his entire ministry. It illumines all the paradoxes and mysteries of his life. In his resurrection not only Jesus is raised from the dead; so is his entire public ministry. Then, for the very first time, it becomes clear who Jesus is and why he taught and lived. Before Easter Sunday, Jesus' true identity had been hidden from his disciples. True, there had been a few occasions when the veil of mystery surrounding Jesus had been briefly lifted. But these had only been momentary flashes of insight. Only after Jesus' resurrection did all of Jesus' works and words begin to make sense.

To understand the Gospels, therefore, we must read them backward. To make sense of the New Testament, we must read it from the perspective of Easter.

Beginning with Sarah

But what about the Old Testament?

Jesus told us how after he rose from the dead. To the two disciples on the road to Emmaus he said, "How foolish you are, and how slow of heart to believe all that the prophets have spoken! Did not the Christ have to suffer these things and then enter his glory?" (Luke 24:25–26). And beginning with the five books of Moses and the prophets, Jesus explained what was said in the Old Testament Scriptures about his death and resurrection.

Jesus offered the two disciples a key to the language of the Old Testament. This monumental explication can be compared to the Rosetta stone, which gave the world the key to the long-forgotten language of ancient Egypt. In 1799, as history relates, an officer in Napoleon's engineering corps found a large rock half buried in the mud near the Rosetta mouth of the Nile. Carved on the stone is a decree by Egyptian priests to commemorate the crowning of Ptolemy V Epiphanes, king of Egypt from 203 to 181 B.C. At the top the text appears in ancient Egyptian hieroglyphics. In the center the text is repeated in the demotic script of spoken Egyptian. At the bottom the same text is written again in Greek.

The language of ancient Egypt written in hieroglyphics had been a riddle to scholars for many centuries. The Rosetta stone solved the riddle. With the help of the parallel Greek text scholars were able to decipher it. A key had been found which opened a hitherto hidden world. The Old Testament too needs a key, for its contents are varied and diverse.

The key is that all these disparate Old Testament stories, Jesus explains to the Emmaus wayfarers, are nothing but tributaries feeding into the mighty stream of his death and resurrection.

How, we wonder, would Jesus have commented on the story of Abraham in Genesis 12. Here God promises Abraham that he will become a great nation and that through him and his descendants all peoples on earth will be blessed. Marvelous! But just a few verses earlier, in Genesis 11, we are told that Abraham's wife Sarah is barren, which makes us wonder what God might possibly have in mind. How can Abraham become a great nation when his wife is barren? Barrenness is dead-endedness, a blind alley. How then can life go on where it has come to an end? God's promise is spoken against the backdrop of barrenness. And we cannot help but wonder: How can God make good on his promise when he chooses such a faulty mechanism as the barrenness of Sarah? There is only one answer. God chooses this route to show that he has power to create new life beyond our dead-endedness.

The resurrection theme also runs silently through the story of Sarah's burial. When Sarah dies the question arises: "Where can her body be buried?" for Abraham is a foreigner with no land holdings. The story tells us that Abraham approaches the city fathers of Hebron and that he asks them, "I am an alien and a stranger among you. Sell me some property for a burial site here so I can bury my dead."

After some negotiating and paying an exorbitant price, Abraham at last becomes the owner of a piece of land where he buries Sarah.

But why bother us with this story? Who cares where Sarah is buried? Why go into such great detail? The answer is that it describes what is central to the faith of God's people. God promised Abraham, as he did Isaac and Jacob, that he would give him possession of the land of Canaan. But he never did. Abraham did live in it but he never possessed it. The only piece he ever owned was a burial plot. Only in death did he enter upon a piece of the promised land that was legally his. This burial site, this dead end, became the meeting place for those who had been promised the land but never possessed it. Here, in death, they met and waited for God to make true his promise, which he did when he raised Jesus from the dead.

Continuing with Jeremiah

How do the Old Testament prophets reflect the light of Jesus' resurrection?

One story that has always intrigued me is found in Jeremiah 32. The situation is this: The kingdom of Judah, the southern kingdom, is on the brink of collapse. The Chaldeans have descended on it like a swarm of locusts, and only Jerusalem is still free. But it is under siege. Jeremiah, God's spokesman, is confined to the guardhouse for having predicted its imminent fall. Then, one day, Jeremiah receives this word from the Lord: "Buy a piece of land!"—which doesn't make sense. With the enemy overrunning the country and Jerusalem about to fall, investing in real estate is sheer folly.

Characteristically, Jeremiah challenges God's command. He files this official protest:

> Here are the siegemounds, raised against the city to storm it; and the city, because of sword and famine and pestilence, is at the mercy of the Chaldeans who are attacking it. What you threatened has come to pass—as You see. Yet You, Lord God, said to me: Buy the land for money and call in witnesses—when the city is at the mercy of the Chaldeans! (Jeremiah 32:24–25 TANAKH)

God's answer is: "Behold I am the Lord, the God of all flesh. Is anything too wondrous for Me?"

In the face of dead-endedness, God commands Jeremiah to have hope. For that is what buying real estate in wartime means—hoping in the future when there appears to be no future. It means trusting that God is able to create new life beyond our dead-endedness.

Resurrection Now

If dead-endedness is our weakness in its most pitiful and naked form, and if resurrection is God's most definitive answer to it, then we next must ask when resurrection comes about. Is it future or present? The answer is both! Resurrection is not just something that will take place at the end of history. It also is a present reality. It comes about each time God creates a new beginning out of the ashes of our lives. Resurrection is totally unforeseeable. It fits Frederick Buechner's description of Donald Duck: "How can Donald Duck foresee that after being run over by the steamroller he will pick himself up on the other side as flat as a pancake for a few seconds but alive and squawking?"

For example, how could the woman with a flow of blood have foreseen that Jesus would raise her from social death? The way Mark tells it (5:21–41), Jesus has just returned from the other side of the Sea of Galilee. Soon the people gather around him and make demands upon him. Jairus, one of the rulers of the synagogue, falls at his feet and begs, "My little daughter is at the point of death. Won't you please come and lay your hands on her, so that she may be well, and live?" Jesus goes with him, followed by a great crowd.

Now if Mark got his stories from Peter, as tradition says he did, then it sounds as if Peter suddenly broke off his story. Another story came flooding back. "Wait a minute," Peter told Mark. "Wait a minute. It was at this point—yes, I remember now. It was at this point that the woman with a flow of blood came up from behind and touched Jesus' garment." And that's how it came about that Mark, in chapter five of his Gospel, tells the story of the woman *within* the story of Jairus. He forgets about Jairus momentarily and continues, "And a woman was there who had been subject to bleeding for twelve years. She had suffered a great deal under the care of many doctors and had spent all she had, yet instead of getting better she grew worse."

She had heard reports about Jesus and comes up behind in the crowd and touches Jesus' garment. "For," she says, "if I touch even his garments, I shall be made well."

Mark wraps the story of the incurably ill woman inside the story of Jairus because these two stories are cut from the same cloth. Both are dead-end stories. The daughter of Jairus dies while Jesus is detained by the woman. While still talking to her, servants come to tell Jairus, "Your daughter is dead." Ignoring them, Jesus goes to Jairus' house, enters the room where the child lies, and speaks to her as though to a sleeping child, "Little girl, I say to you, get up!"

Mark wraps this resurrection story around the story of the woman, as though to say, "This too is a resurrection story." Jesus raises this woman too from death—from social death. For the Mosaic Law barred women with a flow of blood from all social contacts. It considered their condition contagious, just as many of us consider AIDS victims contagious.

Theme with Endless Variations

The story of the woman raised from social dead-endedness has as many variations as there are ways in which the unforeseeable grace of God does impossible things for people in impossible situations, when the water reaches up to our chin or the sky is falling down upon our heads.

I remember the first of such experiences. On May 10, 1940, German troops had invaded Holland. Dutch troops engaged them for five days. To demoralize the population, German radio broadcasts warned that if Holland did not surrender immediately, the *Luftwaffe* would bomb five cities, one of which was Haarlem, my hometown.

It was Sunday afternoon. We had come back from church. My mother had prepared dinner. Now we were all sitting around the dinner table, all eight of us. Then, suddenly, air-raid sirens began their penetrating wailing. This could mean only one thing: German bombers. And I knew: This is the end. The end of me. The end of my family.

I remember dropping my fork and just sitting there, wholly paralyzed by fear. "Let's go stand in the hallway,"

I heard my father say. "They say it's the safest place in the house." So we all made for the hallway, next to the staircase. My heart was pounding, my mouth was dry, I was terrified.

Sometimes, as I seek to live myself into the experiences of Jesus toward the end of his life, in the Garden of Gethsemane and on his way to the place of crucifixion, and as I look for an experience in my own life that in some pale fashion resembles what Jesus went through, so that I can at least come to some understanding of what he suffered, I think of that Sunday afternoon in May of 1940, when as a little boy I was sure that my final hour had struck and that I would soon be torn to pieces by exploding bombs.

When the sirens stopped their wailing, an eerie silence followed. I remember my father saying, "Why don't we pray? There's nothing else we can do." And he prayed that God would save our lives. I have long since forgotten the precise wording of his prayer, except for this one sentence: "We seek refuge in the shadow of your wings, until danger passes"—a quote from Psalm 57.

This sentence hit me with great force and it lit up the dark hallway in which we were standing. Suddenly, from beyond my dead-endedness, a voice assured me that there is a hiding place even when every house in the city lies exposed to death. The words of Psalm 57, charged with resurrection power, wrapped themselves around me. God is a mother hen, I thought, and I am one of her chicks. What can bombs do to me?

Reflecting on this wartime experience, I am struck with how intensely personal the Christian faith is. It is either that—deeply personal—or it is nothing. The Christian faith is not interested in objective descriptions—in the size of God's wings, in the relative humidity beneath those wings, in the velocity of the wind outside those wings. What it is interested in is that I personally experience the warmth and protection of those wings. But to experience these I must first have the daylights scared out of me; I must first have my vulnerability exposed. And until I experience how pitifully weak and helpless I really am, I cannot honestly pray, "Have mercy on me, O God, have mercy on me, for in you my soul takes refuge."

William Willimon, in his book *Sighing for Eden*, writes that when he was in college the late Carlyle Marney came to his college for a religious-emphasis week. Carlyle Marney was a Southern Baptist clergyman, the spiritual mentor of many Southern preachers, but also a maverick—the kind of speaker who was in the habit of throwing curve balls at his audience. So when one of the students asked, "Dr. Marney, tell us what you believe about eternal life," the curt answer he gave was, "I won't talk with you about that."

"Why not?" the students asked.

"Because," Marney said, "there you are at nineteen or twenty, never having known indigestion, heartburn, impotence, defeat. So what can you know of death? Come back at forty-five and we'll talk about eternal life with integrity."

Translation: We can only experience resurrection from a position of dead-endedness. We can only see the risen Jesus through our tears. For people who are well fed, well dressed, well futured, healthy, potent, and gifted, resurrection cannot mean much; such people already have their salvation. What would they need a resurrection for? But for the parent weeping for a prodigal daughter, a widow at thirty with young children, a wife cast aside by her husband, a gay person shunned by his community, a manic depressive, a terminally ill patient—that's a different story!

Marney is right. There is little point in discussing Easter with people who have not experienced Good Friday. The light of the resurrection is not likely to reach people who do not experience the world around them as void of hope. Such people, says Kierkegaard, are like a man riding through the night in a brightly lit carriage. He is incapable of seeing the stars because of the artificial light; he has lost his ability to orient himself to the stars, and with it he has lost his sense of direction.

Journey into Light

To understand the Gospels, then, we must read them with Easter in mind. From beyond each of their stories we must hear the voice of the risen Jesus say to us, "Come to me, all you are weary and burdened, and I will give you rest. Experience my resurrecting power, all you who are stuck in dead-endedness."

For some people dead-endedness is a sudden process; for others a gradual one. Some people's lives are placed in crisis suddenly; some slowly evolve to the point where the people must finally admit their bankruptcy.

Such was the case with Emile Cailliet, who tells the story of his search in his book *Journey Into Light*. Born in a small village in France, Cailliet grew up in a family that was not in the least religious. In the formal education he received there was no room for God. Nature, he was taught, is the sum total of all there is.

His upbringing and education proved of little help when he volunteered in the First World War. The killing and carnage of trench warfare challenged all his views and values. One day a friend of his, while standing in front of him, was killed by a bullet. One night a bullet got him too. An American field ambulance crew saved his life and, later, the use of a badly shattered arm. During his stay at the American Hospital he married a Scotch-Irish girl whom he had met the year before the war had broken out. She was a devout Christian. Cailliet's attitude toward the Christian faith, however, remained unchanged, and he told his wife that Christianity would be taboo in their home. "Little did I realize at the time," he writes, "that a militant attitude often betrays an inner turmoil."

After nine months in the hospital, Cailliet was discharged and resumed his graduate studies. But the books to which he returned were no longer the same books. Nor was his motivation the same motivation. "Reading in literature and philosophy," he writes, "I found myself probing in depth for meaning. During long night watches in the fox-holes I had in a strange way a longing—I must say it, however queer it may sound—for a book that would understand me."

But for all his extensive reading he knew of no such book. So he decided to make one for his own private use out of passages gleaned from different writers that spoke to his condition. He collected these passages in a leather-bound pocketbook that he always carried with him. He was sure that these nuggets of wisdom would lead him from fear and anguish to freedom and joy.

The day arrived when he put the finishing touch to the book that would speak to his condition. It was a beautiful, sunny day. He went out, sat under a tree, and opened his precious anthology. But the more he read the deeper grew his disappointment. Suddenly he realized that this patchwork of quotations wouldn't work for the simple reason that it was of his own making. Behind these passages stood no single authority that addressed him; it was simply Emile Cailliet addressing himself. Cailliet found himself in a dead-end situation. The fragments of his last hope were as numerous as the passages quoted in his leather-bound book.

At that moment his wife, who knew nothing of the project on which her husband had been working, returned home from an afternoon stroll with the baby carriage. It was a hot afternoon, and on her stroll she had followed the main boulevard. Finding it too crowded she turned to a side street. The cobblestones had shaken the carriage so badly that she had wondered what to do. Then she spotted a patch of grass beyond a small archway. It looked so inviting that she went in with the baby for a few minutes of rest.

The patch of grass led to an outside staircase. She climbed it without quite knowing why. At the top she saw a long room, the door to it wide open. So she entered. At the far end a white-haired gentleman was working at a desk. He had not noticed her. Looking around and seeing a carved cross, it dawned on her that she was inside the office of a Huguenot church building hidden away as they all are, even long after persecution had ceased. The gentleman was the pastor.

She walked over to his desk and then heard herself ask, "Do you have a Bible in French?" He smiled and handed her one.

Now she stood in front of her husband, Bible in hand and remembering the religious taboo governing their home. She meant to apologize, but Cailliet was not interested in her apology. He felt strangely drawn to the book she was holding. "A Bible, you say? Where is it? Show me. I have never seen one before!"

She handed it to him, and he literally grabbed the book and rushed to his study. "I opened it," Cailliet remembers, "and 'chanced' upon the Beatitudes! I read, and read, and read—now aloud with an indescribable warmth surging within. . . . I could not find words to express my awe and wonder. And suddenly the realization dawned on me: This *was* the Book that would understand me! . . . I continued to read deeply into the night, mostly from the gospels. And lo and behold, as I looked through them, the One of whom they spoke, the One who spoke and acted in them, became alive to me."

Emile Cailliet's story is uniquely his own. Yet it is not a unique story at all. His is the experience of countless other Christians who, from the other side of their dead-endedness, suddenly heard a voice promising a new beginning.

4

GOD OF WILDERNESS

One of Leo Tolstoi's most powerful short stories is entitled "How Much Land Does a Man Need?" The hero of this story is Pakhom, a small farmer with one basic grievance—he has too little land. One day, he learns of a new settlement beyond the Volga where one can buy as much land as one has money to pay, so he decides to seek his fortune in this new place. Here he makes out much better. Gradually he acquires more and more land, but not enough to satisfy him.

Then, when he hears that in the country of the Bashkirs there is plenty of land available at a cheap price, he leaves his family at home and with his servant travels three hundred miles to investigate. Soon after reaching the Bashkir camp, Pakhom enters into negotiations with the Bashkir chief.

"What is your price for the land?" Pakhom asks.

"Only a thousand rubles per day," the chief answers.

"How many acres would that include?" Pakhom inquires, for he does not understand this day rate at all.

"We do not reckon in that way," says the chief. "We sell only by the day. That is to say, as much land as you can walk around in a day, that much land is yours. That is our measure, and the price is a thousand rubles."

"Why," Pakhom says in an astonished voice, "a man might walk round a great deal in a day."

"He might indeed," the chief says, "but let me warn you about one thing. If on that same day you do not return to the spot where you started, you lose your thousand rubles."

"It's a deal," Pakhom says, whose mind is made up to mark out a very large Promised Land the next day.

Before sunrise the next day Pakhom and his servant and the Bashkir chief with some of his men go to a hill overlooking a vast area of grassland. There the chief takes off his cap, lays it down, and says, "This will be the mark. Lay your money in it and have your servant remain beside it while you are gone. From this mark you will start and to this mark you will return."

Pakhom takes out his money, lays it in the cap, and then prepares himself to start. "I will walk toward the rising sun," he decides.

No sooner does the sun send its first rays across the horizon than Pakhom starts walking into the steppe, a couple of mounted Bashkir men riding behind him to plant stakes wherever Pakhom decides to have them. After a couple of miles Pakhom grows warm and begins shedding some of his clothes. Later, when it really gets hot, he takes off his long boots. "Walking without them will be easier," he tells himself. On and on he walks. Far beyond the point where he should have turned north, but the farther east he goes the better the land becomes. He's beginning to tire now. Glancing at the sun he sees that it is time for lunch. He eats some bread but without sitting down. "Once I sit down I'm likely to lie down and fall asleep."

He goes on again. At first he finds walking easy, for the meal has revived his strength. But soon the sun seems to grow all the hotter. Pakhom is almost worn out now, but keeps telling himself: "An hour's pain may be a century gain." As he is about to head west he spots an excellent piece of land. "It would be a pity to leave that out," he thinks, so he continues north for a while.

It's getting late now and Pakhom has to be back before sunset. So he finally heads south. "I must hurry straight back now, otherwise I won't make it back in time." His feet are aching badly. From time to time he staggers. There is such a long way to go yet. Pakhom pulls himself together and breaks into a run. On and on he runs. Now he can hear the Bashkirs cheering him on. He can see the cap and the chief sitting beside it. Pakhom reaches the hill just as the large red sun touches the earth. He scrambles up the slope. Then he stumbles and falls. While falling he stretches out his hand toward the cap and touches it.

"Ah, young man," the chief cries, "you have earned much land indeed!"

Pakhom does not hear, for when his servant tries to raise him he finds that Pakhom is dead.

After a while the chief gets up, takes a spade from the ground, throws it to Pakhom's servant, and says, "Bury him!"

After the Bashkirs have left the servant buries his master in a small plot of land—just big enough for his body.

The temptation of land, Tolstoi is saying, is greed. People never have enough. They always want more. Their capacity for unhappiness is as great as there is land in the world. People crave land because it represents power. The more land, the more power; the more power, the more security; the more security, the less need for dependence on God.

How significant therefore that God chooses the desert as the cradle of his servants. God commands Abraham, for instance, to leave Ur of Chaldees, a place where springs are plentiful and rains pour from heaven and pastures are alive with sheep and cattle, and to go south to the Negev region where all is desert, the rainfall slight, and pasture land poor.

Abraham makes Beersheba his base. Beyond Beersheba the deserts begin—the Judean Desert to the north, the Wilderness of Paran to the south, and the Desert of Shur to the west. Here, enclosed by deserts, Abraham lives off his livestock—sheep, goats, cattle, camels, and asses. He pastures his goats on the lower slope of Mount Hebron to the north. The other animals he brings down to the plains of Negev, where they must constantly move from one place to the next.

Isaac and Jacob keep away from the populated areas in the north and, like Abraham, move from place to place, pasturing their livestock in the hill country between Shechem and Hebron and in the arid plains of Negev.

The people of Israel too are formed in this kind of environment. The wilderness journey from Egypt to the Promised Land is not just a passing interim between bondage and freedom. Rather, it is the cradle of their birth as a nation under God and the home of their upbringing. Here they learn that Yahweh is first and foremost a God of wilderness. Here they come to experience their own weakness and helplessness and their dependence on God.

Israel cannot be God's servant people without the wilderness experience. With its heat by day, its cold by night, with its dryness and barrenness, the wilderness is so imperious in what it does to people and allows so little of what people can do for themselves, that it is an ideal place for God to make and mold his people. Here life is constantly on the brink of death. Here people are so deeply aware of their powerlessness, so utterly at the mercy of outside help, that what they do is nothing and what God does is everything. As Harry Emerson Fosdick once put it, "The wilderness is the best place on earth in which to be a Calvinist."

The wilderness is a place where there is no visible supply of water, bread, and meat. It is the absence of all human aid and comfort. It is the place par excellence to "worry about your life, what you will eat or drink." But it is also the place where, just when you think yourselves forgotten and abandoned, you come face to face with the daily faithfulness of God.

God of Daily Bread

There are two ways to find out what bread is—the scientific route or the experiential route. You can study bread or you can taste it.

What is true of bread is true also of people. You can find out what someone is like by studying, interviewing, and psychoanalyzing, by reading his or her diary, by observing that person in a family situation. Or you can befriend or marry that person.

Furthermore, what is true of bread and people is true also of God. You can read about him in the creeds and in books of theology, or you can get to know God by becoming involved with him, by arguing with him like Job, by wrestling with him like Jacob, by praying to him like Daniel, and by living with him in the desert for forty years like Israel. You can learn about God with your mind or through your experience. God prefers the latter. He wants us to know him experientially, to engage him with our whole lives.

Which explains why, after God liberates his people from slavery, he sends them into the wilderness. For the wilderness is the place to get to know God. Here the people of Israel learn the lesson of dependence on God. The wilderness is a place that shows us our weaknesses. It's a place where all the conventional and convenient support systems break down.

We Westerners have nearly mastered the art of controlling nature. We open a faucet and water flows. We flip a switch and there is light. We turn up the thermostat and the temperature goes up. We turn it down and the temperature drops. In the wilderness it is just the other way around. Here we don't control anything; everything controls us. That's why God prefers the wilderness as a place of instruction. Where we get to know God best is not in a setting where meals are served at set hours but in places where all the supports of human civilization are stripped away so that we wonder where in the world our next meal is going to come from.

When the people of Israel wonder about where their food will come from and when they complain bitterly, God promises to deliver manna the next morning. He meets their request, not to stop their complaining but to teach them what kind of God he is. *"Man yu?"* the people ask. "What is it?" For the word *manna* is not so much a name as it is a question or an expression of amazement. Israel receives in the wilderness what it thought was only available in Egypt. It receives bread from an economy it does not know.

The people must learn two things about God. First, that he provides bread, and second, that he does so on a regular basis.

Alyoshka, a character in Aleksandr Solzhenitsyn's novel *One Day in the Life of Ivan Denisovich,* is one of those who has learned this lesson in the wilderness of a Soviet work camp. Condemned to twenty-five years of hard labor, Alyoshka is strangely unaffected by the terror and torment of his wilderness environment. The prison camp does not worry him. It's like water off a duck's back. As a Baptist Christian, Alyoshka receives daily strength from a notebook into which he has copied half the Gospels. Because he is so clever at hiding this book, it has never been found on any of the searches.

One day, as Alyoshka is reading the Gospels, he turns to his neighbor, Ivan Denisovich Shukhov, and says, "Look here, Ivan Denisovich, your soul wants to pray to God, so why don't you let it have its way?"

Shukhov sighs, "I'll tell you why, Alyoshka. Because all these prayers are like the complaints we send in to the higher-ups—either they don't get there or they come back to you marked 'Rejected.' With all your prayers, are you any better off than we are? We all got twenty-five years, because that's how it is now—twenty-five years for everybody."

"But I don't pray for that, Ivan Denisovich," Alyoshka says, and he goes up close to Shukhov with his Gospels, right up to his face. "The only thing of this earth the Lord has ordered us to pray for is our daily bread— 'Give us this day our daily bread.'"

Israel must learn what Alyoshka has learned, that all food comes from God and that he parcels it out in daily portions. The daily bread God provides is very much like God himself. He does not allow us to claim him. He is with us on his terms, not ours. He zealously guards his freedom, yet he is not capricious. He can always be relied upon. Furthermore, you can never possess and store the food that God provides. When you do, it begins to smell. For God does not allow us to control it, just as he does not allow us to control him. Still, God does not dispense his manna capriciously. It does not rain down one day and not the next. As God's gift it is renewed every morning. And this daily wilderness miracle Israel must always remember.

Remember or Perish

In an address delivered at Northwestern University in 1977, Elie Wiesel reminded his audience: "I belong to a people that remembers. No other people remembers as well both our friends and our enemies as we do. . . . Just as all the days were created for one day alone, the Sabbath, all the other words were created and given the one word alone, 'Remember.'"

Whether it be its most recent or its most ancient past, Israel remembers. Why? Not merely to recollect what once happened to it, but to wake up to it, to be renewed by recalling it. Israel remembers because it believes that God speaks to his people, not directly, but through its remembered past. When Israel has come to the end of its wilderness journey and as it is about to cross over the Jordan into the Promised Land, God tells it to remember.

Why must Israel remember at this particular time? Because crossing over the Jordan is one of the most critical moments in Israel's life. What could be more critical for it than to pass from land not sown to land that is sown? No transition is more radical than that of sojourners becoming possessors.

Before Israel takes this momentous step, God invites it to look back over the past forty years and reflect on "the vast and dreadful desert, that thirsty and waterless land, with its venomous snakes and scorpions" and how the Lord gave "manna to eat in the desert" and "brought water out of hard rock" (Deuteronomy 8:15–16). Israel must always remember that its life in the wilderness was a life on the brink of death. It must always remember that it was weak and only God was strong, that God shielded it, cared for it, and guarded it as the apple of his eye.

When Israel remembers, it will have its hope restored. For God is not capricious. What he did in days past he will do also in days to come. Israel must hand down to generations to come the remembrances of its wilderness experiences so that they too may be inspired with power for living. Israel must remember its wilderness sojourn right before crossing over the Jordan because the Promised Land is like the wilderness. In the Promised Land, Israel need not worry either about what it shall eat or drink. Here too God will dispense food and drink on a daily basis.

Yet there is a significant difference. In the Promised Land, God's gifts are not as direct and spectacular as they were during wilderness days. Here they are indirect and natural. Here food does not fall from the sky but grows in fields and hangs from trees. Here water does not come gushing from rocks but flows from wells. Here therefore the ultimate giver of all good gifts is easily lost sight of. The gift can easily become divorced from the giver. The produce of the land can easily be mistaken as the fruit of human labor, and the land can easily be treated as human property. The more they are, the stronger Israel will feel, the less dependent on God.

What resources does Israel have to resist these

temptations? Its chief resource is remembering and, in remembering, to hear again the voice of its God.

Church of the Wilderness

Like early Israel, the early church spent its formative years in a wilderness—the Roman Empire. The early Christians saw themselves as pilgrims longing for a better country. On their way "they went about in sheepskins and goatskins, destitute, persecuted and mistreated. . . . They wandered in deserts and mountains, and in caves and holes in the ground" (Hebrews 11:37–38).

The Book of Revelation also views the church as a wilderness church. In Chapter 12 a pregnant woman, arrayed with the symbols of eternity and heavenly majesty, cries out in the pain of bringing forth a child. Mixed through her pain, however, is the joy of anticipation. Something new is about to be born: a male child "who will rule all the nations with an iron scepter."

This woman is Israel. The child to which she is about to give birth is Jesus. This child has an enemy: a great red dragon, which elsewhere in Scripture is called the Devil and Satan. It was God's enemy from the beginning and is now the enemy of Jesus. The dragon tries in vain to devour Jesus who, in an apocalyptic moment, is caught up to God and to his throne.

With only a short time in which to exert its power, the dragon now turns on the woman and goes in pursuit of her. But the woman is given two great eagle's wings to fly to the place in the wilderness where she will be sustained and where she will be out of the dragon's reach.

Frustrated, the dragon decides to wage war on the rest of the woman's offspring—the church of the wilderness, "those who obey God's commandments and hold to the testimony of Jesus." The initial phase of this war lasted from the end of the first century to the beginning of the fourth. During this time Christians endured the hostile climate of persecution and were deprived of many of the benefits that Roman civilization provided.

The focal point of Roman hostility was first of all the matter of emperor worship. Roman authorities were basically tolerant in religious matters, allowing each nation under their jurisdiction to practice its own beliefs. No religious community was persecuted so long as it obeyed imperial law. The only point on which the authorities were uncompromising was that of emperor worship, which was a matter of imperial law. And when it came to law—any law—the authorities permitted no laxity.

The early Christians paid taxes, prayed for the emperor, and avoided all political provocation. But they refused to recognize the emperor as divine or worship his image. And this refusal eventually became the reason for persecution. Well known are the words of the aged Bishop Polycarp of Smyrna. In an effort to save Polycarp's life in A.D. 156, the chief of police said to him: "What is there after all in calling upon the lord emperor, sacrificing to him, and all the rest? Think of your grey hairs, swear by the divine spirit of the emperor and I shall set you free; only curse Christ."

Polycarp's answer was: "Eighty-six years I have served him, and he has never done me any wrong. How can I bring myself to blaspheme my king who has saved me?"

Less known but equally moving is the testimony of Julius, an army veteran. Julius was arrested during the last and most severe persecution under Diocletian, who was emperor from A.D. 284 to 305. Diocletian ordered all churches to be burnt down and all Christians holding state office to be fired. He also ordered all Christian leaders to be imprisoned and that all other Christians, and this included Julius, make offerings to the emperor at the penalty of death.

After being led before the governor, the governor told Julius: "What is there to it? You scatter a little incense and go home." But Julius's answer was: "I am an old soldier, and in twenty-seven years of service I was never accused of any fault, not even a quarrel. I went through seven campaigns and was never found wanting. The emperor discharged me with honor. And now do you want me, who was faithful in the least, to be unfaithful in the greatest thing of all? I have always feared God and now I am ready for my last service."

Emperor worship united the innumerable peoples and religions of the Roman world under a single banner: "One Empire, One Faith." Those who refused to worship the emperor thereby placed themselves outside the pale of Roman law and order, and soon found themselves living in a wildernesslike environment.

The wilderness through which the early Christians sojourned was also moral in nature. Paul's assessment of first-century current morality is not overstated. Paul says nothing that Greek and Roman writers of that age do not say themselves. It was an age of unparalleled immorality. In this *Playboy* society of permissive morality, the behavior of the early Christians stood out like light in darkness. In the words of Aristides, a second-century Greek Christian, Christians "do not commit adultery or fornication, nor bear false witness, nor embezzle what is held in pledge, nor covet what is not theirs. They honor father and mother, and show kindness to those near to them; and whenever they are judges, they judge uprightly."

The testimony of an unknown second- or third-century Christian sounds much the same. Christians, he writes, "marry as do all people; they bear children, but they do not abandon their offspring. They furnish a common table, but not a common bed. Their lot is cast 'in the flesh,' but they do not live 'according to the flesh.'"

Leaving the Wilderness

After Emperor Constantine converted to the Christian faith, the church received unlimited freedom. The battle between church and state was over. No longer were Christians persecuted for their faith. But not without paying a great price for this freedom. Having been unable to destroy the church, the Roman state now befriended it. What it needed from the church was a spiritual cement to hold the empire together. Constantine had witnessed the heroic behavior of Christians under persecution, and he knew they could not be wiped out by violence. War with them would only disrupt the Empire. He therefore stopped the persecutions and made peace with the church, thereby setting in motion a process from which eventually a state church would emerge.

This abrupt reversal of events had drastic consequences. Whereas before being a Christian required great courage, now for many it became a matter of calculation. Whereas before the road to career advancement led past the imperial altar, now it led past the baptismal font. The world came flocking into the church and the church was not prepared to deal with this mass influx. It lacked the personnel to instruct and christianize the pagan masses entering through her doors. The world entered the church and there lived on as the world but now under a Christian disguise. Church and state became intertwined, the church serving the unity of the state and the state taking an active part in preserving the unity of the church.

The days of wilderness sojourning with the church's total dependence on the power of God were over. Increasingly Christians drew upon an alien power—the Roman state and civilization. Sojourners turned into settlers. Christendom was born.

The most eloquent and incisive critic of Christendom was the Danish thinker and writer Søren Kierkegaard (1813–55).

What Christianity demands, Kierkegaard wrote satirically, is chastity—to do away with the whorehouse. In Christendom the whorehouse remains what it is in paganism, but it has become a "Christian" whorehouse.

What Christianity demands is honesty and fair dealing, to do away with swindling. In Christendom, swindling remains what it is in paganism, but it has become "Christian" swindling and hides behind such slogans as "Business Is Business."

And so in everything. Christianity drives us into wilderness living. It makes us realize how empty our personal resources are, how fragile our support systems, how unreliable our attachments, and how for everything we depend on the grace and power of God. Christendom Christianity allows us to leave the wilderness. It allows us to draw strength from alien sources.

Try to imagine, Kierkegaard wrote in his diary, that geese can talk and conduct worship services. Every Sunday they meet and listen to the gander's sermon. The gander preaches on the high goal for which God has created them. They are to use their wings to fly to distant lands where they really belong, for they are only strangers on earth.

The gander may preach all he wants but nothing changes. The geese eat and drink and grow fat. While their conversations on Sundays are extremely serious, on Mondays they have no use for the geese who take flying seriously. "It's all because they can't think of anything but flying that they lose weight and grow pale and don't enjoy God's blessings like we do," they say.

Next Sunday they go to church again, and the old gander preaches again about the glorious end for which God has destined them and for which he has given them their wings. And it is just the same with Christendom worship.

What Christians must do to deserve the name Christian, Kierkegaard says, is to live the way the wood pigeon first lived. Once, so his parable goes, there was a wood pigeon. He had his nest among the tall, straight trees of a wood where wonder and excitement dwell together.

Not far away, where the smoke rises from the

farmer's house, lived some tame pigeons. The wood pigeon would often meet a pair of these tame pigeons. He would sit on a branch, which spread out over the farm, and they on the ridge of the roof. One day they were talking about food. The wood pigeon said, "I never worry about food. Each day I find enough food to stay alive. That's how I get through life."

The tame pigeons answered, "With us it is different. With us the future is secure. At harvest time the farmer hauls in many loads of corn—enough to feed us for a long, long time."

After the wood pigeon returned to his nest he did some serious thinking. It must be a nice feeling, he thought, to know that there is enough food stored up to last you for a long time. Maybe I should begin to gather amounts of food and store them in secure places.

The next day he awoke earlier than usual and was so busy gathering food that he hardly had time to eat. But each time he went back to his secret storage places he found that the food was gone, that other animals had eaten what he had gathered.

A great change came over him. Though he found his food every day as before, he still was not satisfied. What he suffered was not want but anticipation of want in the future. His peace was gone. He had discovered anxiety about the necessities of life.

"This securing of the future is constantly on my mind," he said. "Oh, why am I a poor wood pigeon and not one of the tame ones?"

At last he could take it no longer and flew off to the farmer's house. Here he mixed in with the tame pigeons. He noticed a place where they flew in, so he too flew in, for there, no doubt, was the storehouse.

That evening, when the farmer came home and closed the pigeon loft, he discovered the wood pigeon. He put it in a little cage by itself till the next day. Then he killed it and thereby released it from worry about the necessities of life!

Pigeon-loft Christianity is really the opposite of wilderness Christianity. For it lives off a different food. And it seeks to live under a different security arrangement. It seeks the best of two worlds but remains a stranger to both.

5

GOD OF MADNESS

In 1965, while visiting the Soviet Union, Elie Wiesel attended a synagogue service on the eve of Yom Kippur. The synagogue was crowded. What struck Wiesel was that all the men were elderly and defeated-looking. Nor was the rabbi, whose face spoke of resignation, an exception. He seemed to be living elsewhere, in a faraway past.

Then a "what if" idea occurred to Wiesel. What if the rabbi suddenly stepped out of the past, pounded the pulpit, spoke out, said what oppressed him, shouted his pain, his anger, his truth? What if?

But nothing of the sort happened. For the old rabbi it was too late. He had seen too much, suffered too much. He symbolized the tragic isolation of the Russian Jews persecuted and humiliated from the time of the pogroms to the reign of terror under Stalin.

During the weeks after his visit to Russia, Wiesel decided to write a play in which the old rabbi is given a chance to redeem himself. The title Wiesel gave to the play is *Zalmen, or The Madness of God*. It takes place in a small-town synagogue somewhere in Russia in the late fifties, in post-Stalin times when deportees are returning from Siberia but when fear and silence continue to mark the life of Jewish communities. Nobody as yet is brave enough to denounce the evils of the past and to demand freedom and dignity now.

In Wiesel's play, Zalmen the beadle tries to coax a

timid and fearful rabbi into protesting the persecutions at the forthcoming synagogue service when a group of twelve foreign actors, whose bus broke down, will be present. Even though only four of the actors are Jewish, all express the wish to attend the local synagogue service.

At an emergency session, the synagogue council decides not to use this foreign presence as an occasion to provoke the authorities. The council chairman reminds everyone: "We have managed to survive innumerable persecutions over the centuries. How did we do it? We learned to wait, to exercise restraint. Waiting was a necessity for us and we turned it into an art. . . . Therefore, I say we must accept and endure and—don't be shocked—collaborate. Or at least, play the game of collaboration."

Zalmen, however, has a different opinion. He wants his rabbi to become mad. "Break the chains, Rabbi! Let your anger explode! This is your chance. A chance offered by God. Don't let it slip away. If you do, you're a coward!"

"A coward or simply a man trapped by habit?" the rabbi asks. "Is it our fault we have forgotten how to walk alone, how to take risks, how to venture forth on unknown paths? Can you condemn us for that? It's not courage we lack, but knowledge. Some elementary notions were erased from our minds. We no longer know how to do or undo certain things—we have forgotten how to shout, how to vent our anger, how to say no."

"You lack imagination, Rabbi! And that's unforgivable. For we are the imagination and madness of the world—we are imagination gone mad. One has to be mad today to believe in God and in man. One has to be mad today to believe. One has to be mad to want to remain human. Be mad, Rabbi, be mad! Become a rabbi once more. A shepherd. A leader who points the way. A keeper of the flame. A smasher of idols."

That evening the seed Zalmen planted in his rabbi's mind bears fruit. At the appropriate time, the rabbi gets up, positions himself behind the pulpit, and announces: "We proclaim ourselves free from false promises, from vows taken under duress. What we have said is now unsaid. We aspire to a moment of truth, and if that truth shall bring us nothing but tears, so be it. But our bonds shall not be bonds and only by our tears shall we abide. I say and proclaim: that is more than we can bear!

"You, our foreign brothers who see us now, hear the last cries of a shattered community! To you I say: the sparks are dying, and our heritage, our very destiny are covered with dust. Broken are the wings of the eagle, the lion is ill. And I say and I proclaim to any one who will listen that the Torah here is in peril and the spirit of a whole people is being crushed. And all the sufferings, the faith, the obstinate and desperate courage, the allegiance to a covenant three thousand years old, will have been for nothing.

"If we allow this to continue, if you, our brothers, forsake us, we will be the last Jews in this land, the last witness, the last of the Jews who in silence bury the Jew within them. And know this, brothers who leave without having spoken to us, that so much silence is breaking my heart, that hope has deserted me. Know that it is more than I can bear, it is more than I can bear."

God at His Wheel

Mad people like the rabbi roam the pages of Wiesel's writings. To us they seem strange. They say crazy things and do crazy things. They live out of a different vision and challenge the established order in the name of that vision. They speak a truth many have forgotten and all need to hear. They ask such questions as: "What if you have your values reversed?" "What if the people you call sane are really mad?"

The subtitle of Wiesel's play, however, is not *The Madness of Zalmen* or *The Madness of the Rabbi*, but *The Madness of God*. The rabbi's madness is derivative. The original madness is God's. And God's madness is his decision to choose a weak and despised people to be the instrument of his saving purpose in history, to be the means whereby he brings healing and salvation to the nations. God's madness is that he brings his cause to victory through the people of Israel.

The same idea is presented in Scripture. Isaiah 43:8–13 suggests a cosmic trial. The scene is that of an international court in which different parties present their testimony. The question to be decided is: Which god has shown himself to be lord of history by giving events their true interpretation before they ever happened?

God first challenges the Gentile nations to present their testimony. But not a single witness steps forward. Then God turns to Israel and says, "You are *my* witnesses. Tell the nations what I have done for you. Tell them that I am a God who saves, that I, I am the Lord, and besides me there is no savior."

In God's international court only one issue must be resolved, only one question must be answered: "Who among the gods of the nations has power to save?" Israel's task in history is to answer that question. Answering that question constitutes its calling.

The madness of God is to choose the Jews—a people of pitiful weakness, a people despised and rejected—to be his witness. The madness of God is his decision to be present where least expected and to speak where least likely to be heard. The madness of God is to display his power and glory in a place least likely to be looked for—a vessel of clay.

To acquaint Jeremiah with his madness, God tells him to visit a potter's house and watch him working at his wheel. What Jeremiah sees is that the clay makes no shape for itself, except crazy shapes, ugly shapes, useless shapes. What he sees is how the true life of the clay only spins into symmetry under the potter's hands.

As Jeremiah stands watching the potter, something goes wrong. The potter is not satisfied with his work. The vase he is working on turns out not quite symmetrical. He wonders: What will the potter do now? Swear under his breath, take the lump of clay and throw it at his dog, and then go out and drown his frustration in a pitcher of wine?

No, he reworks it into another vase. And suddenly it occurs to Jeremiah that what he is watching is a parable of God's patient and skillful molding of Israel over the centuries. There is never a moment for the clay when the potter is not doing something with it. No sooner has one work gone bad than his fingers are pressing it into the form of another. God is never standing back and watching Israel. His fingers are on his people all the time, for although they are called to be his servants and in some measure are responding, yet at the same time they are always rebelling against the claims that this servant role makes upon them and are constantly seeking a less demanding destiny for themselves. The service that Israel offers to God has ever been and ever remains a broken service.

From every side God touches and presses. If Israel obeys his will, God is pleased. If it is rebellious, his fingers oppose and knead it back into shape. God kneads, presses, pushes, and pulls. He never gives up. He never discards what is ruined. He re-uses it. *That* constitutes God's madness.

The Self-Chosen

The people of Israel are often called God's chosen people. Meaning what? Being chosen in the Bible means being recruited for a task, being deputized. God is the recruiter, the deputizer. No one else can do this. No people can choose itself. God chose Abraham and, in him, Israel. Why Abraham? Why Israel? We will never know. The only thing we do know is the task for which God chose them: "Abraham will surely become a great and powerful nation, and all nations on earth will be blessed through him" (Genesis 18:18).

At one time or another, other peoples too have claimed to have been chosen by God—chosen to bless others. The pre-war Japanese, for example, made this claim.

The reason Japan was so fanatically dedicated to what it called its "holy war" in East Asia was that it believed itself to have been chosen by God to be the savior of the Far-Eastern world, to share with nations less fortunate than herself the blessings of her culture. The imperial edict of September 27, 1940, announcing the ratification of the Three-Power Pact between Germany, Italy, and Japan, for example, opens with these words: "To enhance justice on earth and make of the world one household is the great injunction, bequeathed by our imperial ancestors, which we lay to heart day and night."

Japan is not the only nation to have claimed divine chosenness. The Netherlands, Germany, France, and England, to mention but a few, all have, in their days of military and economic strength, claimed the same thing. In the days before the Second World War, I grew up with the slogan "God, Nederland, en Oranje" (God, the Netherlands, and the House of Orange), which was the Dutch version of the Three-Power Pact.

The idea of chosenness is also deeply rooted in the American consciousness. Americans have often drawn parallels between their nation and Israel. As God has led the people of Israel through the wilderness to the Promised Land, so, the early Americans felt, God had led them to the New World. In his Second Inaugural Address, for example, Lincoln stated: "I shall need, too, the favor of the Being in whose hands we are, who led our fathers, as Israel of old, from their native land and planted them in a country flowing with all the necessities and comforts of life."

This America-Israel parallel is but one step removed from claiming that God chose America to bless all peoples on earth. The early Billy Graham took this step. According to William G. McLoughlin in his book *Billy Graham: Revivalist in a Secular Age*, the Graham of the fifties linked Christianity and the American way of life as represented by free enterprise capitalism. Russia was the evil empire, guided by Satan, and the United States was the last hope of the world and of Christianity against Communism. World War III, presumably the final battle between God and Satan, would be between Russia and the United States.

In many of Graham's sermons of that era the United States represents the forces of good and Russia the forces of evil. "I believe that America is truly the last bulwark of Christian civilization," Graham preached in 1952. And two years later: "I am more impressed than ever with America's responsibility in this complex world. We might as well face it; there is a war on in the world for the minds of the human race." While he deplored all the corruption, crime, and moral decay in American society, Graham declared nevertheless that "this is still the greatest country in the world" and that "we were created for a spiritual mission among the nations."

So spoke Billy Graham in the fifties. No longer does he speak that way, though other evangelical leaders still do. As recently as 1980, Jerry Falwell claimed that God chose the United States from among the nations to be the principal bearer of the Gospel. While it is true "that God could use any nation or means possible to spread the Gospel to the world, it is also true that we have the churches, the schools, the young people, and the means of spreading the Gospel worldwide in our lifetime."

We meet, however, the crassest and crudest example of self-chosenness in Nazi ideology. The Aryans, Adolf Hitler claims in his book *Mein Kampf*, are the chief bearers of human cultural development. Why? Because of their willingness to sacrifice personal achievement and if necessary their own lives for others. In the lower breeds of people this self-sacrificing quality is present only to a very small degree, so that often they do not go beyond the formation of the family. The Aryans differ from all other people by their willingness to enlist all their abilities in the service of the larger human community.

The strongest counterpart to the Aryans, Hitler claims, are the Jews. In them the instinct of self-preservation is developed most strongly. The best proof of this is the mere fact of their survival. Jews lack completely the most essential requirement for a cultured people. In the Jewish people the will to self-sacrifice is limited to the individual's naked instinct of self-preservation. Jews, therefore, possess no culture-creating force of any kind. The Jew, wrote Hitler, "is and remains the typical parasite, a sponger who like a noxious bacillus keeps spreading as soon as a favorable medium invites him. And the effect of his existence is also like that of spongers: wherever he appears, the host people dies out after a shorter or longer period."

Not the Jews but the Aryans, Hitler claims, are the divinely chosen people to bless the world. As a central act of this blessing activity, every Jew everywhere in Europe had to be killed. Seventy-two percent of them were, as the following grim statistics show:

Country	Jewish Population Sept. 1939	Jews killed	Percentage of Jewish Deaths
1. Poland	3,300,000	2,800,000	85
2. USSR (occupied)	2,100,000	1,500,000	71.4
3. Romania	850,000	425,000	50
4. Hungary	404,000	200,000	49.5
5. Czechoslovakia	315,000	260,000	82.5
6. France	300,000	90,000	30
7. Germany	210,000	170,000	81
8. Lithuania	150,000	135,000	90
9. Holland	150,000	90,000	60
10. Latvia	95,000	85,000	89.5
11. Belgium	90,000	40,000	44.4
12. Greece	75,000	60,000	80

Country	Jewish Population Sept. 1939	Jews killed	Percentage of Jewish Deaths
13. Yugoslavia	75,000	55,000	73.3
14. Austria	60,000	40,000	66.6
15. Italy	57,000	15,000	26.3
16. Bulgaria	50,000	7,000	14
17. Others	20,000	6,000	30
Total:	8,301,000	5,978,000	72

The God-Chosen

In the chapter "God of Weak Partners" I asked: Why did God choose Israel as his partner? Why, to bless all peoples on earth, did God decide to work through a people of negligible strength and no repute?

Next we focused on the Christian church and wondered: Is the church cut from the same cloth as Israel? Do both church and Israel belong to the things in this world that are weak and despised?

What we did not ask is: How are Israel and the church related? Who are presently the chosen people of God? Jews as well as Christians? Or have the Christians displaced the Jews? This madness of God to bless all peoples on earth through the Jews, is it still operative? Or did Israel merely function as a rocket that lifted the church into its orbit around the world, so that the Jewish people would now be floating through time and space like a spent force?

For many centuries, almost from the beginning of its history, the church has maintained that as the new Israel she has displaced the original Israel as the people through whom God blesses all peoples. She has claimed that with the coming of Jesus and the founding of the church, Israel concluded its mission in history.

Over the centuries this theory, the so-called displacement theory, has fostered a climate of anti-semitism. "As a child," Elie Wiesel recalls, "I was afraid of the church to the point of changing sidewalks. In my town, the fear was justified. Not only because of what I inherited—our collective memory—but also because of the simple fact that twice a year, at Easter and Christmas, Jewish schoolchildren would be beaten up by their Christian neighbors. Yes, as a child I lived in fear. A symbol of compassion and love to Christians, the cross has become an instrument of torment and terror to be used against Jews. I say this with neither hate nor anger. I say this because it is true. Born in suffering, Christianity became a source and pretext of suffering to others."

The history of Christianity is a history marked throughout by anti-semitism. Nazi anti-semitism, while anti-Christian, would have been impossible without centuries of Christian anti-semitism.

To believe and teach that the role of old Israel is finished and that God has relegated his former partner to the limbo of history, of course, has criminal implications that people with criminal minds are certain to spell out in time. Which is precisely what the Nazis did when they ordered that all Jews without exception were to be destroyed.

There can be no question that the Christians were one link in the chain of events that led to the Holocaust, a chain that Raul Hilberg in his book *The Destruction of the European Jews* describes as conversion, exile, and extermination: "The missionaries of Christianity had said in effect: You have no right to live among us as Jews. The secular rulers who followed had proclaimed: You have no right to live among us. The German Nazis at last decreed: You have no right to live."

The Holocaust and the legacy of anti-semitism, much of it Christian in origin, leading up to it, have led many Christians and churches to rethink their relationship to the Jewish people. They have begun asking questions such as:

—Why has the Christian way always been presented as having superseded the way of Israel?

—Haven't Christians, with their centuries-long history of dehumanizing Jews and with their complicity in the Holocaust, denied Jesus the Christ just as much as they accuse the Jews of having done?

—If Jesus had been at Auschwitz, would he have been found among the Christians, the executioners, or among the Jews, the victims?

—Why didn't Hitler encounter any significant Christian opposition to his policy? Why were Catholics and Protestants alike part of a thundering silence that assured Hitler that he could continue his slaughter of the Jews with impunity?

—Is it possible to believe the Christian Gospel in a way that honors and makes room for the Jewish people?

—Isn't a breach with the Jewish people a breaking away from God's plan for the fullness of time to reunify all of humankind?

Because many Christians and churches have begun to struggle with questions such as these, some amazing changes have come about in the last third of our century. The position taken by the Second Vatican Council represents one of these changes. Low in pain and anguish and repentance though it may be, it at least initiates a fresh look at the Jewish people. With an appeal to what Paul writes in Romans 9–11, it confesses that the church cannot forget "that she draws sustenance from the root of that well-cultivated olive tree [Israel] onto which have been grafted the wild shoots, the Gentiles." It also clears the Jews of the charge of deicide. What "happened in Christ's passion cannot be charged against all the Jews, without distinction, then alive, nor against the Jews of today. Although the church is the new People of God, the Jews should not be presented as rejected or accursed by God, as if this followed from the Holy Scriptures."

There can be no doubt that we have entered a new era of Christian-Jewish relationships. Instead of the displacement theory we now hear the opinion that the present-day Jews are still God's chosen people.

Instead of hearing that the church has displaced the Jews as the people of God, we now hear that, since Christ, the one people of God is broken asunder, one part being the church that accepts Jesus as the Messiah, the other part being Israel outside the church, which rejects him but even in its rejection remains the people of God's first call.

Chapters 9 through 11 of Paul's letter to the Romans is receiving fresh attention. For centuries only individuals and sectarian groups concerned themselves seriously with this part of Paul's message. The church and its theologians were mainly interested in that part of Romans 9 that seemed to be important for the dogma of predestination. Now, however, many Christians and churches have begun to ask themselves what it means that God's call or choosing of Israel is irrevocable (Romans 11:29).

What Paul saw happening in his day was that the church was increasingly becoming a Gentile church and that church and synagogue each were going their separate ways. This development, to Paul, was a great mystery. For he firmly believed that it was God's plan for the fullness of time to unite all people, to unite Jews and Gentiles. Why then did Israel go its own way? Did this mean that it was dropping out of God's plan, that it had finished its role in the drama of salvation and was now walking off the stage? Did this mean that Israel could escape from its chosenness, that it could get from under the responsibilities that chosenness brought with it?

Suppose Israel were able to do this. Suppose Israel were able to walk away from its chosenness. This would mean that not God but Israel had the final word. It would mean that Israel could unilaterally terminate its partnership with God.

Israel, however, did not and does not have this

option. God's partnership with Israel is an everlasting partnership. "Only if the heavens above can be measured and the foundations of the earth below be searched out will I reject all the descendants of Israel because of all they have done," declares God in Jeremiah 31:37.

Israel's refusal of Jesus as the Messiah, says Paul, does not mean that it drops out of God's plan. Rather it is part of that plan. There is mystery in Israel's refusal to recognize Jesus as the Messiah, a mystery that is guided by God himself.

That mystery is the same mystery we meet in Jesus' parable of the Prodigal Son. This parable, which is often read from an individual perspective, can also be interpreted as embracing all people, both Jews and Gentiles.

The father is God the Father. The two sons are Israel and the Gentiles. The elder son is Israel. He is challenged to accept his younger brother, the Gentiles. He is asked to accept the Gentiles as children of his father, to live with them in the same house, and to feast with them at the same table.

The younger son is the Gentile church. He is challenged to be grateful to the elder brother, not to exalt himself arrogantly over him, but to learn from him.

These are God's two sons, and in Jesus' parable we see how God deals with them, how he loves both, how he does not prefer one over the other nor disown one in favor of the other.

The behavior of these two sons makes God decide to embark on a course of action that strikes us as sheer madness. Instead of exercising his fatherly power he decides to deal with his sons from an attitude of powerlessness.

The father is almighty. He can say to the younger son: "I refuse to give you what you ask for." He can say anything he wants and do anything he wants. Yet he assumes the role of someone who is totally powerless, for he knows that if he exerts his power he will lose his son.

The real shock, however, comes in the final verse of

the parable. The elder son stands outside and refuses to join the party. The people of Israel refuse to recognize Jesus as their Messiah.

Where is the father? At the banquet table? No! He is out in the darkness where his elder son is boiling over with anger and jealousy.

Now the father is almighty. He can call on some of his servants to force his son into the banquet hall. But he does not do that. He decides to treat his elder son the same way he treated his younger son, from a position of weakness.

The parable therefore ends the same way that Romans 9–11 ends, with the younger son enjoying food and drink and dancing, and with the powerless almighty father out in the darkness, pleading with the elder son to join him and his good-for-nothing Gentile brother.

That's the most surprising feature of this story: the attitude of the father who does not force his sons against their will and yet draws both of them gradually toward himself by his great love.

6

GOD OF POVERTY

Is God partial? Does he side with the poor against the rich? Is he a God of the poor? Can we only understand the Bible when we read it with the eyes of the poor?

These questions are very much in the Christian news. An emerging consensus in certain Christian circles seems to be that God has a bias in favor of the poor, that their interests have his attention over the interests of the rich and that Christians should reflect this divine bias in the way they live.

On the other side of the spectrum is mass-media evangelicalism with its impeccably dressed guests and celebrities who testify that God has blessed them with success and wealth. The image of American evangelicalism, wrote Jim Wallis, "is a religion for those at the top, not those at the bottom of the world system. . . . Evangelicals are known to have a decided preference for the successful and prosperous who see their wealth as a sign of God's favor."

Which of these positions, biblically speaking, is correct? Should our lifestyles show us to be people who stand with the poor and side with the oppressed, or should a concern for the poor not cramp our success-oriented way of living? What does Jesus mean in Luke 6:20 when he says, "Blessed are you who are poor, for yours is the kingdom of God"?

Some Bible versions translate instead, "Happy are the poor," but this is not helpful. Being blessed is not the same as being happy. You can be blessed without being happy and you can be happy without being blessed. Blessings come to us from above. They are objective. Happiness originates from below. It is subjective.

The opposite of blessed, therefore, is not unhappy, but woeful. "Blessed are you who are poor . . . but woe to you who are rich," Jesus says in Luke 6. For the rich, he seems to say, have nothing to look forward to; they already have what they want. At best, the future can only be an improved version of the present.

But the poor are different. They are blessed. They have a future. Theirs is the kingdom of God.

Who Are the Poor?

Does Jesus mean the economically poor, the poor in money? Yes, but not necessarily. It is easy to oversimplify matters by reducing poverty to a material fact. This is wrong, for someone who is rich in money can be poor in spirit, and someone poor in money can be rich in spirit. Material poverty is an economic condition, and economic conditions as such have no redemptive value. If they did, we would have to promote rather than combat poverty.

Who, then, are the poor whom Jesus pronounces blessed? They are those whom the Old Testament prophets and psalmists call the *anawim*. The word *anawim* is a plural form of the Hebrew word *anaw* and has been variously translated as "the poor," "the humble," and "the afflicted."

The Isaian passage (61:1) Jesus chose as the text for his inaugural sermon tells us who these *anawim* are: "The Spirit of the Sovereign Lord is on me, because the Lord has anointed me to preach good news to the poor [*anawim*]. He has sent me to bind up the brokenhearted, to proclaim freedom for the captives and release for the prisoners."

The *anawim* are the poor, the brokenhearted, the captives, and the prisoners. They are people full of despair—despair of people, despair of the high and mighty whose mouths are full of vacuous promises. Above all, the *anawim* despair of themselves, like the priest Don Emmanuel in Miguel de Unamuno's short story "Saint Emmanuel the Good, Martyr."

The narrator of the story is a devout country girl by the name of Angela. In Angela's eyes, Don Emmanuel is a saint. As village priest, his life consists in patching up poor marriages, in talking rebellious children into submitting to their parents, and above all in comforting the embittered, the brokenhearted, and the dying.

The marvel of Don Emmanuel is his voice, a voice so beautiful that it brings people to the brink of weeping. On Good Friday, when he intones Jesus' dying words, "My God, my God, why hast thou forsaken me?" a wave of emotion passes through the congregation. It is as if they are hearing the voice of Jesus himself.

Everyone in the village, some thousand people, attends church, even if only to hear and see Don Emmanuel. Here they recite the Apostles' Creed in unison, making the thousand voices sound as one: "I believe in God, the Almighty Father, Creator of heaven and earth . . ." As they reach the article "I believe in the resurrection of the body and the life everlasting," however, the voice of Don Emmanuel falls strangely silent. It drowns in the unison voice of the people. To Don Emmanuel, this confessed future appears as a land of deep darkness. From it no light shines on him.

Don Emmanuel shuns contemplation. He has a deep fear for having to think in solitude. He spends his life in action—chopping wood for the poor in winter, accompanying the doctor on his rounds to add his prestige to the doctor's prescription. Relentlessly, he flees from solitude into activity.

Some of his most-loved words are those he once spoke at a wedding: "Ah, if I could only change all the water in our lake into wine, into a dear little wine which, no matter how much of it one drank, would always make one joyful without intoxicating, or, if intoxicating, would make one joyfully drunk."

But below the surface of Don Emmanuel's joyousness runs the strong current of sadness that he conceals from the eyes and ears of his parishioners. "I am put here to give life to the souls of my charges, to make them happy, to make them dream they are immortal—and not to destroy them," he once explains to Angela's brother Lazarus. His task "consists in consoling myself by consoling others, even though the consolation I give them is not ever mine."

Pointing to the nearby lake one day he says to Lazarus: "There lies my direst temptation. How that water beckons me in its deep quiet! My life, Lazarus, is a kind of continual suicide, or a struggle against suicide, which is the same thing. . . . Just as long as our people go on living!"

Don Emmanuel, who is racked by doubt and thinks he does not believe, who by his sacrificial living creates hope in people's lives but thinks himself excluded from that hope, mirrors the fate of all the *anawim*. The *anawim* derive little comfort from their home-grown resources. They constantly struggle against the dark whirlpool deep down inside of them that slowly consumes all their inner strength.

The *anawim* are not necessarily poor in money. The economically poor can still have their pride or their dreams or their religion. The *anawim,* on the other hand, have learned that not much needs to happen for all these props to disintegrate before their eyes.

There is, however, something else. Mixed in with their despair is the yeast of hope. The life of the *anawim* is a curious mixture of despair and hope. It constantly moves between these two poles. Though they despair, yet their hope never dies. The *anawim,* says Isaiah (50:10), walk in darkness and have no light, yet they trust in the name of the Lord.

What sparks their hope and keeps it burning is the

voice of God. They hear this voice and are haunted by it. Though they are distrustful of it because it promises such fantastic things, things they can only think of in their wildest dreams, they at the same time hopefully think: "But who knows what will happen when, once more, all things will be going God's way."

A Poor Man's Prayer

Hughes Oliphant Old writes that, like many devout Jews of his day, Jesus knew most of the psalms by heart. The Book of The Psalms was his prayerbook. In the Upper Room, after the Last Supper, Jesus sang the Hallel, that is, Psalms 113–118, with his disciples. On the cross he prayed Psalm 22, and in the Garden of Gethsemane he meditated on Psalms 42 and 43, praying them three times.

Why Psalms 42 and 43? Because they reflect the agonizing conflict of the *anawim* faith. For example, in Psalm 42:9 the psalmist prays, "I say to God my Rock . . ."

Now, let's suppose that Psalm 42 abruptly ended at this point. "I say to God my Rock . . ." Let's suppose further that *you* would be asked to finish writing the psalm. How would you finish it? You would be tempted, would you not, to write something along these lines: "I say to God my Rock: 'In you I take refuge.'"

The way the psalmist continues is quite different: "I say to God my Rock, 'Why have you forgotten me?'" First he confesses God to be his rock, his place of refuge. Then in the same breath he accusingly asks God: If indeed you are my rock, why don't you behave like one? Why do you shake beneath me?

This is typical *anawim* language, mixing despair and hope.

God's promises are like stars. Above us are billions of stars, not just at night but also during the day. Objectively speaking, these stars are always there, day and night. Only, we are not always able to see them. The daylight disables us from seeing them. For us to see them, it first must turn dark. So it is with God's promises. To see them, to derive comfort from them, the lights around us first must go out.

This is what is happening in Psalms 42 and 43. The lights are going out and in the deepening darkness the poet lifts up his eyes in hope:

Why are you downcast, O my soul?
　Why so disturbed within me?
Put your hope in God,
　for I will yet praise him,
　my Savior and my God.

It is precisely when every human avenue has been explored and found wanting, when every help from human sources has been sought but has not been forthcoming, that the light of God's promises shines brightest and that Jesus' words, "Blessed are you who are poor, for yours is the kingdom of God," provide most comfort.

During the early period of the Reformation, when persecutions swept over large sections of Europe, Christians used to hide their Bibles in cavities of walls, being careful to cover them with bricks and mortar. Centuries later some of the Bibles were recovered. When experts examined them they made an amazing discovery. They found that the passages spelling out God's greatest promises were least legible.

What accounts for this? The tears of sixteenth-century *anawim* that had dropped on these passages.

Poverty—A State of Mind

Of all the people he pronounces blessed, Jesus puts the poor at the top of his list. Why? Why not begin with the hungry or the meek? Because poverty is the gate through which we enter God's world. To leave our world and enter God's we must get out of our egos and learn to listen to someone besides ourselves.

Poverty is not one of the many Christian qualities we must possess. Rather, it is the essential quality of being accessible to God. Poverty separates the sheep from the goats. If you are rich, rich in the sense of self-sufficiency and self-will, there's little God can do with you. You are not pliable.

The *anawim*, on the other hand, are. They stand before God weak and vulnerable, but also ready to do his bidding. They tremble at his word and allow themselves to be pruned by it.

Poverty in the Bible is a frame of mind, not first of all an economic condition or a question of money. It's a question rather of the heart.

Economic poverty, by itself, is not a virtue. After all, you can be dirt poor and yet be as greedy as the man in Jesus' parable who tore down his barns and built bigger ones to store all his grain and his goods.

And then again, you can be a person of means and yet have the soul of a pauper.

To be poor is to be weak before God, to be open to him. God doesn't need strong people. He prefers working through the poor in spirit. Not through the poor as such, but through those whose poverty makes them receptive to him.

These poor can also be found among the rich, for there is a poverty of body as well as a poverty of soul. Each evokes God's pity. God loves everyone, even those who are well-off. It's just that he has a much harder time getting through to them.

Parade of *Anawim*

These *anawim*, who are the opposite of self-made and self-sufficient people, who find no comfort in their own resources, and who are in far worse shape than the poor in money who, after all, still can have their pride or their dreams or their religion—what do flesh and blood *anawim* look like? What kind of lives do they live? By what names are they known to us?

Abraham. Leading the *anawim* parade is Abraham who at a number of occasions experienced that strange mixture of despair and hope, but never more intensely than when God told him to sacrifice his son, Isaac. For by sacrificing his son, Abraham sacrificed himself, sacrificed everything he believed in, everything he hoped for. If Isaac were to die, what would become of the future God had promised? Can you imagine a deeper despair than thinking, "I shall have lived and suffered for nothing"?

God's command is Abraham's despair, not his tragedy. For the story of Abraham and Isaac is not tragic.

In Greek mythology there is a parallel story that *is* tragic. A thousand ships carrying the Greek army lie ready to sail in Aulis, a place of strong winds and dangerous tides, impossible to sail from as long as the north wind is blowing. The only way to calm the wind is to appease her by sacrificing to her a royal maiden, Iphigenia, the eldest daughter of the commander-in-chief, Agamemnon.

Agamemnon is caught on the horns of a tragic dilemma. Shall he act for the good of his family or for that of the state? His ambition as military commander wins out over the love for his family, and he sends home for his daughter: He writes his wife that he has arranged a great marriage for her.

Trusting her father, Iphigenia comes to her wedding but is carried to the altar instead and killed. As she dies the north wind ceases to blow.

Upon his return home Agamemnon must pay with his life. His wife strikes him dead, punishing him for the murder of his own child.

Abraham's story of sacrificing Isaac is not tragic in that sense. In Abraham's case it is not a matter of choosing between two conflicting values but one of choosing between the fear of God and disobedience.

"Now I know that you fear God," the angel says to Abraham when he is about to slay his son. The test is whether Abraham is open to God's Word even in the most trying circumstances, whether he still hopes in God when everything around him has turned to darkness.

Who else belongs to the *anawim*? *Elie Wiesel*. Born in 1928, Elie Wiesel grew up in Hungary, somewhere in the Carpathian mountains. His dreams were filled with God, prayer, and song. Then in April of 1944 he and his family and all the Jews of his town were rounded up like cattle and deported to Auschwitz. They arrived at midnight. The guards said, "Men to the left! Women to the right!"

As he stood with his father, wondering whether his mother and sisters would come back, someone told him the truth: "Do you see that chimney over there? Do you see those flames? Over there—that's where you're going to be taken. That's your grave, over there. Haven't you realized it yet? You're going to be burned. Frizzled away. Turned to ashes."

The young Elie turned to his father and said, "It is impossible. I don't believe it. It cannot be. It has to be a lie. This cannot be happening, not in the heart of civilized Europe, not in the middle of the twentieth century. The world would not remain silent."

In his book *Night*, a memoir of his concentration-camp experiences, Wiesel describes his despair in what have become perhaps the most frequently quoted words from classic Holocaust literature:

> Never shall I forget that night, the first night in the camp, which has turned my life into one long night, seven times cursed and seven times sealed.
>
> Never shall I forget that smoke.
>
> Never shall I forget the little faces of the children, whose bodies I saw turned into wreaths of smoke beneath a silent blue sky.
>
> Never shall I forget those flames which consumed my faith forever.

Never shall I forget that nocturnal silence which deprived me, for all eternity, of the desire to live.

Never shall I forget those moments which murdered my God and my soul and turned my dreams to dust.

Never shall I forget these things, even if I am condemned to live as long as God Himself. Never.

Ever since that first night, Wiesel has been torn between two irreconcilable realities—that of God and that of Auschwitz. Each seems to cancel out the other, and either refuses to disappear. The darkness is never total, for there is God. But neither is the light of God's presence strong enough to dispel the darkness.

Hope never completely disappeared from Wiesel's life. The voice of Israel's God never completely grew silent. It became audible again, first softly in his next book *Dawn*, and then, somewhat louder, in such later books as *Messengers from God* in which he wrote about biblical characters and their meaning for today's living.

Abraham. Elie Wiesel. Who else? *Mary*—the mother of Jesus.

If you were to meet Mary, would you recognize her? What adjectives describe her? Is she beatific and beautiful? Is she meek and mild? Is she poetic and pious?

Do any of these words bring Mary into focus for you? If you think they do, take a fresh look at her Magnificat (Luke 1:46–55). The child to which I am about to give birth, Mary sings, will be an agent of radical social and political reform. He will liberate people from oppression, famine, and poverty. He will change the face of human society. He will erase the inequities accumulated over the centuries, so that everybody will begin again at the same point.

Mary is definitely not the sweet young lady she's often been portrayed to be. She talks of social and political changes. She prophesies that the child in her womb will be the greatest revolutionary of all times.

In the October 3, 1977, issue of *Christianity and Crisis*, Robert McAfee Brown wrote an article in the form of a dialogue between a Roman Catholic priest and some of his destitute parishioners. The setting is a country in Central America where there has been a brutal persecution of church leaders and where a number of priests have cast their lot with the poor—the *anawim*.

It is Sunday morning and one of these priests conducts an informal service somewhere.

"Father," one of the parishioners points out, "today is the Feast of the Holy Name of Mary!"

"Is there any connection between Mary and Martin Luther King?" the priest asks.

"Well, there would be if Mary was concerned about the oppressed people."

The priest replies: "Let me read part of Mary's Song, the part that says, 'He has scattered those who are proud in their inmost thoughts. He has brought down rulers from their thrones but has lifted up the humble. He has filled the hungry with good things but has sent the rich empty away.'"

"But Father," the parishioner reacts, "that doesn't at all sound like the Mary we hear about in the cathedral. And the Mary in the 'holy pictures' certainly doesn't look like someone who would talk that way."

"Tell us about the Mary in the holy pictures," the priest invites.

The parishioner displays one and says, "Here she is. She is standing on a crescent moon. She is wearing a crown. She has rings on her fingers. She has on a blue robe embroidered with gold."

"That does sound like a different Mary from the Mary of the Song," the priest says. "Do you think the picture has betrayed the Mary of the Song?"

"The Mary who said 'God has lifted up the humble'

would not have left all of her friends so she could stand on the moon," comes a response.

"Right!" everybody agrees. "Take her off the moon!"

Then someone else says: "The Mary who said that 'God has brought down rulers from their thrones' would not be wearing a crown."

"Right!" everybody says. "Take off her crown!"

Then someone else says: "The Mary who said that God 'has sent the rich empty away' would not be wearing rings on her fingers."

"Right! Take off her rings!"

Someone in the corner says: "The Mary who said that God 'has filled the hungry with good things' would not have left the people who are still hungry, to wear a silk robe embroidered with gold."

"Right! everybody agrees. "Take off her robe!"

"Okay," the priest says, "if you don't like the way Mary looks in this picture, what, do you think, does she look like?"

"She would not be standing on the moon. She would be standing in the dirt and dust where we stand," someone volunteers.

"She would not be wearing a crown. She would have on an old hat like the rest of us, to keep the sun from causing her to faint," someone else says.

"She would not be wearing rings on her fingers. She would have rough hands, like ours."

"She would not be wearing a silk robe embroidered with gold. She would be wearing old clothes like the rest of us."

Then an embarrassed parishioner says: "Father . . . it may be awful to say this, but it sounds as though Mary would look just like me! My feet are dirty, my hat is old, my hands are rough, and my clothes are torn."

Mary, spokeswoman of the *anawim*!

Abraham, Elie Wiesel, Mary. Who else?

Martin Luther. Shortly before his death, Luther wrote these words on a piece of paper: "No one ought to think that he has sufficiently tasted of the Scriptures, even if, for a hundred years, he has governed the church along with such prophets as Elijah and Elisha, John the Baptist, Christ, and the apostles. We are all beggars. That's the truth."

Luther translated the entire Scriptures into the German language. Almost single-handedly he changed the course of European history. Yet, standing before God, this exceptionally talented man despaired: "We are all beggars."

Abraham, Wiesel, Mary, Luther. Who else?

Kaj Munk. Carlyle Marney, in a speech addressed to the Princeton Theological Institute, makes a distinction between what he calls "cellar people" and "balcony people." Cellar people are people chained to the past, he said, people adjusted to their culture, in love with the latest fashion, impressed by their culture's heroes and stars and celebrities.

Balcony people are people on the way. They have not, but they hope for. They see not, but they obey. Their road is not defined, but is a permanent venture. It is created under their feet. They look at the cellar people and despair. They listen to God's voice and have their hope renewed. They are constantly torn between despair and hope. Yet they are our stimulators, our encouragers, our prodders, our critics, our mentors.

Danish pastor and playwright Kaj Munk was one of these balcony people. Already in his first sermon, preached in 1919 as a student, Munk has Jesus confront the Danish cellar people of his day. "His eyes search for the weak and the desperate, but they are no longer there. In all of their eyes he reads self-conscious and self-willed pride. A great sorrow fills his hearts. He remembers his ancient word once spoken in discouragement: 'When the Son of Man comes, will he find faith on the earth?' . . . What Jesus sees is the great desertion. Human society, though it officially honors his ideas, in reality has kissed them goodbye."

This voice—Munk's voice—also speaks through some of the characters in his plays. It speaks, for example, through Johannes in Munk's play *The Word*.

The leading character is Mikkel Borgen, a modern Danish farmer who, like Jacob in the Book of Genesis, is always a few steps ahead of God and always telling God how to bless him.

Some of the other characters are young Mikkel, Borgen's eldest son, who seems to have no faith at all, and his wife Inger, who is expecting a baby any day now. And the new Lutheran pastor who, though he does not deny that God can perform miracles, does not believe that he ever does. Then there is the doctor who only believes in himself and in his scientific knowledge and the miracles it can work. Finally, there is also Johannes, Borgen's second son.

What brings all of these people together is Inger's sudden death. Something goes terribly wrong during the delivery. The baby's life has to be sacrificed to save that of the mother. But that same night Inger dies as well.

Five days later all are together in Mikkel Borgen's large living room. Inger is laid out in a coffin. After all have said farewell to her, Borgen says, "Now—the lid." But Johannes protests: "No—not the lid! Is this a Christian funeral? Where is the sure and certain hope of resurrection?"

"But Johannes!" his father pleads, "We are poor mortals of little account."

"That's blasphemy: to be poor and little, when we have so rich and great a God. Here you all stand, as defenseless in the face of death as naked nestlings in the cat's claw of fate. You cling to your flimsy heathenish conjectures and your home-made human consolations. And yet it was for you that Christ lived, died and rose again."

"That's all quite true, Johannes," his father says, "but it's so difficult all the same."

"I know it is. But if you hadn't enough Christian

blood in you to count on the triumph of Easter, you might at least have had the courage of prayer and have asked God whether you might have Inger back. That hasn't occurred to a single one of you. . . . Is there really nobody? Not a single one of you to support me, while I pray for a miracle to come down on us? I tell you—all things are possible to him who believes."

Then Maren, young Mikkel and Inger's daughter, slips her hand into his, and rekindles Johannes's faith. "The child!" he says. "The greatest in the kingdom of heaven! I forgot *you*. Yes, yes—salvation is with the child. . . . Now then, little girl, look at your mother. When I call on the name of Jesus, she will rise up. Now look at her, child. And, next, I shall command you, you dead—"

At this point the pastor protests: "This is scandalous. Miracles can't happen nowadays. Both from the ethical and religious—"

"Hypocrite!" Johannes interrupts. "Will you unwittingly do Satan's errand in the guise of godliness? You're crippling my power. You have always persecuted prophets and stoned apostles. Away with you!"

"I'll not move. I stand here in virtue of my office," the pastor answers.

"Very well, then. Stay here to represent the State— but not God." And then Johannes prays, "Hear me, O Father above. Give me the Word—the Word that Christ brought down to us from heaven—the creative, quickening Word of life. Give it to me *now!*" And to Inger he says, "Hear me, you that are dead. In the name of Jesus, who overthrew the grave—if God will, come back to life! I say to you—woman, arise."

Then, as once at the tomb of Lazarus, the greatest of all miracles happens. The dead woman opens her eyes and speaks.

Even so, doubts remain. "But this—it's a physical impossibility. It just can't happen," the pastor mumbles.

And the doctor adds, "These amateur death certificates must be done away with."

God's good news is too good to be true.

The Really Poor

The really poor is Christ, for he who had always been God by nature did not cling to his prerogatives as God's equal, but emptied himself, stripped himself of all privilege by consenting to be a suffering servant and to be born in human likeness (Philippians 2:6–7).

In his book *Philosophical Fragments*, Kierkegaard explains the meaning of Christ's emptying himself with a simple story. A king falls in love with a humble maiden. How should the king declare his love to her? Should he elevate her to his level? Should he show himself to her in all his kingly glory? If he were to do so, he would totally overwhelm her. And suppose she were to respond to the king's love, would there not always linger in the king's mind the suspicion that it was not he whom she loved but his power and riches?

To get around this problem, the king might disguise himself as a beggar and so approach the girl. But this would introduce a new problem. Suppose that as beggar he managed to win her love, she would then love a beggar and not a king.

Nor would it do, instead of lowering himself to a beggar, to elevate the girl instead. For it would suggest that the humble maiden is not good enough to be loved on her own terms, whereas it is precisely as a humble maiden that the king loves her.

The only solution is for the king actually to become a beggar, not merely to pretend to be one, and so seek to win the maiden's love.

This is what happened when Christ emptied himself and became a human being. He actually became something that he had never been before: poor. That's why God made him so rich afterward.

As Christ became poor before God made him rich, so as Christ's followers we must first become poor in spirit before God will give us his kingdom.

"Blessed are you who are poor, for yours is the kingdom of God."

7

GOD OF PAIN

God of *deep* pain, that is. God of the kind of pain to which there is no answer, only a reply. God of the kind of pain that is unfair, unnecessary, and undeserved. God of the kind of pain Don Wanderhope suffers in Peter De Vries's novel *The Blood of the Lamb*.

Don Wanderhope

Wanderhope is a pun on the Dutch word *wanhoop*, meaning despair. As the story of Don Wanderhope's life develops, each of his hopes turns into *wanhoop*.

Don grows up in a strict Calvinist community and mildly manic household. His father is a doubter who constantly fluctuates between faith and reason. His older brother Louie, whom he adores, is an avowed atheist. Louie's death at the age of twenty triggers Don's loss of faith.

Don marries Greta, an old girlfriend. They have a child, a girl. But after a religious conversion, alcoholism, a series of hospitalizations and attempted suicides, Greta finally manages to take her own life.

Death, which has taken from him the two persons he has ever loved—his older brother and his wife—now reaches for his eleven-year-old daughter Carol and strikes her with leukemia.

During the ordeal of hospital visits Don returns to some measure of his childhood faith. On his way to the hospital one day he stops in the Church of St. Catherine to sit down and rest, his head "numbed by the plague of voices in eternal disputation."

After a while he gets up and goes to the rear corner, to the shrine of St. Jude, Patron of Lost Causes and Hopeless Cases. There he sinks to the floor and prays, "I do not ask that she be spared for me, but that her life be spared to her. Or give us a year. We will spend it as we have the last, missing nothing. We will mark the dance of every hour between the snowdrop and the snow: crocus to tulip to violet to iris to rose. . . . All this we ask, with the remission of our sins, in Christ's name. Amen."

That morning the marrow report is encouraging. A nurse tells him, "Practically normal. Carol's in remission."

On his next visit Don carries a cake with Carol's name on it. On his way to the hospital he turns into the church of St. Catherine, sets the cake down on an empty pew and joins the kneeling figures.

On the way out he talks to Mrs. Morano, the night nurse.

"You heard about Carol," Don says.

"Yes, it's exciting. That's why I'm so sorry about this."

"What?"

"The infection. It's been going through the ward like wildfire. Half the kids are in oxygen tents."

"Carol?"

Mrs. Morano nods. "They had me phone you this morning but you'd left."

Don hurries to the hospital. One look at Carol and he knows it is time to say good-bye. Her foul enemy, "that sluggishly multiplying anarchy," has his will of her at last.

While taking Carol's blood pressure, the nurse whispers, "Almost none at all. It's just as well. Only a matter of hours now at the most."

After the nurse leaves, Don moves to Carol's side and

whispers to her the final benediction he remembers from his boyhood days: "The Lord bless thee, and keep thee; The Lord make his face shine upon thee, and be gracious unto thee; The Lord lift up his countenance upon thee, and give thee peace."

Then he touches the stigmata one by one—the prints of the needle, the wound in the breast, caresses her head, and kisses the cheeks and the breasts that would now never be fulfilled. "Oh, my lamb."

At three o'clock in the afternoon Carol dies.

Passing the church of St. Catherine on the way to the car, Don remembers the cake. It is still where he left it that morning, untouched.

Outside again, he pauses on the sidewalk, turns around and looks up at the figure of the crucified Christ above the central doorway. Then he takes the cake out of the box, balances it on the palm of his hand, draws back his arm, and lets fly with all his might.

The cake hits its target, just beneath the crown of thorns. A cry of despair, of defiance: "If you are so powerful, why did you allow this slaughter of the innocent?"

Days later, going through the things in Carol's room, Don finds a statement of his philosophy of life he once wrote in response to a college alumni questionnaire. He finds that it still reflects the way he thinks: "I believe that man must learn to live without those consolations called religious, which his own intelligence must by now have told him belong to the childhood of the race. . . . Man has only his own two feet to stand on, his own trinity to see him through: Reason, Courage, and Grace. And the first plus the second equals the third." With this salute in the direction of the human mind and heart, the story of Don Wanderhope ends.

When we suffer deep pain we can make a reply, as Don Wanderhope did when he flung the cake at the Christ image and when he reaffirmed his faith in reason and courage. But we cannot come up with an answer.

In his book *Gravity and Grace,* Joseph Sittler explains the difference between the two, between answer and reply. He uses the example of a child waking up in the middle of the night and telling the mother coming into the room, "I'm scared."

The mother says, "There's nothing to be afraid of. There's nothing under your bed. There's nothing in your closet."

"I know," says the child, "but I'm still scared," for deep fear is stubborn.

The mother does not answer the child's fear. She does not even try to answer it. Any wise mother says, "Don't be afraid, I'm here." That's not an answer to the child's fear but a reply to it.

Christianity has no answer for deep pain. All it has is a reply, a concrete way of dealing with it. There *can* never be an answer to it, for deep pain enmeshes us in evil, and evil is and always will be a mystery. Deep pain is simply there, for us to reply to. Either defiantly, the way Don Wanderhope did, or stoically or submissively or even joyfully. It all depends on the vision of God we take with us into the shadows. It all depends on how we perceive God's power and love to work in our life.

We're so easily victimized in times of pain. For we bring with us certain notions of what ought and ought not to happen. When these expectations are disappointed we easily give way to defiance or resentment or else sink down into despair. "Why? What kind of God are you?"

One year after I left seminary, I preached a sermon in which I used the metaphor of embroidery. On the wrong side of it, so I explained, all we see is a tangled mess of loose threads of various lengths. Nothing makes sense. But one day God will show us the other side with the beautiful design he has been stitching all along. Then we will see that even the most painful experiences are part of a harmonious whole.

My text (you guessed it) was Romans 8:28 in the King

James Version: "All things work together for good to them that love God."

But do they? Do all things work together for our good? Does leukemia? Does the death of a young mother? Does chronic depression or mental illness? Paul, fortunately, does not say they do. He says, rather, that "in all things God works for the good of those who love him" (NIV). God works for our good *in* all things and *through* all things, no matter how awful and painful. But the sum total of these evil things does not add up to something good.

There is no answer to the problem of deep pain for there is no explanation of evil. Job's comforters, as you may recall, seek to explain Job's suffering to him. They say that Job's suffering is deserved punishment for his sins. Job, however, persists in his claim that he is innocent. But if he is innocent, why does God allow him to suffer?

The answer Job finally receives, if you can call it that, is that there really is no answer. None of Job's questions is answered. Nothing is even said about suffering and justice. In the new perspective God opens to Job's eyes, the question "Why do I suffer?" has lost its urgency. How foolish of Job to deduce from his limited experience that the whole universe is unjustly governed! Has Job the wisdom to know what justice encompasses in universal terms and face to face with the great mystery of evil? Does Job have the wisdom to judge all people with a more authentic justice than God's?

The Book of Job concludes with a prayer of confession in which Job accepts the mystery of God's justice:

"I know that you can do all things;
  no plan of yours can be thwarted . . .
Surely I spoke of things I did not understand,
things too wonderful for me to know."

The heart of the whole problem is the problem of God's power. If God is almighty—as the Bible says he is—and if God is love—as the Bible says he is—then why doesn't he exercise his power in a loving manner? Then why does he appear weak? Then why does he allow innocent children to be slaughtered by killer diseases?

This is Don Wanderhope's parting question as he lands the cake with Carol's name on it smack in Christ's face.

John Claypool

In the late sixties John Claypool went through an experience similar to that of fictional Don Wanderhope, although John took with him into the valley of the shadow of death a different vision of God.

In July of 1968, his eight-year-old daughter, Laura Lue, was diagnosed with acute leukemia. She lived eighteen months and ten days from the time of diagnosis. During those months Claypool preached three sermons in which he shared this experience with his congregation— the Crescent Hill Baptist Church in Louisville, Kentucky. In 1974 he published these in a booklet entitled *Tracks of a Fellow Struggler*.

The most revealing of these sermons is the one preached after his daughter's relapse some nine months after the diagnosis. His text was from Isaiah 40 (RSV):

> He gives power to the faint,
>   and to him who has no might he increases
>   strength.
> Even youths shall faint and be weary,
>   and young men shall fall exhausted;
> but they who wait for the LORD shall renew their
>   strength,
>   they shall mount up with wings like eagles,
> they shall run and not be weary,
>   they shall walk and not faint.

How you make out when the bottom drops out, Claypool told his congregation, depends on the particular vision of God you take with you into the depths. The way you respond to deep pain is going to hinge largely on how you perceive God's power to come to you in those depths.

God's power may come in the form of ecstasy, through the experience of mounting up with wings like eagles. If we wait for the Lord, we will be able to soar, to rise above our normal vantage point, and see things more nearly the way God sees them. Ecstasy provides us with a vantage point above ground level.

The woman who poured costly perfume on Jesus' head had such a vantage point. What she saw caused her to be so wasteful that it made the ground-level disciples gasp: "Why this waste of perfume? It could have been sold for more than a year's wages and the money given to the poor" (Mark 14:4–5).

Soaring with wings like eagles is a valid form of religious experience. But it is not the only form God's power can take. "There has been no ecstasy in the last two weeks," Claypool reported to his congregation. "How could there have been? Laura Lue suffered more intensely than ever before. . . . In that kind of setting— standing by a bed with a little child moaning and thinking the night would never end—ecstasy is not only inappropriate, it is downright impossible."

Isaiah therefore says that God's strength can also take the form of energy to do a job or to solve a problem or get on with some task. "They shall run and not be weary." This is another way in which to experience God's power. Our faith can motivate us and empower us to get busy with a project that needs doing.

But energy for action is no more the totality of Christian experience than ecstasy is. It isn't the only way we experience God' power. For there are times when you are far from running, when there is no room to run, when you can do nothing to change the situation. "We were doing everything we knew to do—leaving no stone unturned, no avenue untried—and still she lay there crying and the problem persisted. If I had been the kind of person who looked to God for 'answers' or programs of activity that had to lead to concrete solutions," Claypool said, "I would once again have been frustrated. . . . There was simply no room 'to run and not be weary.'"

Fortunately Isaiah describes still another form that God's power can assume; namely, endurance—the strength to walk and not tire. In some ways, this may look like the least desirable of the three forms of divine strength. For who wants to be slowed down to a walk, just barely above consciousness level? So that, if the prophet had submitted Isaiah 40:31 to me and had said, "This is the outline of a sermon I plan to preach. What do you think of it?" I would have suggested that he reverse the order. First, they shall walk and not faint. Then, they shall run and not be weary. And finally, they shall mount up with wings like eagles. That way, so I would have pointed out, you work up toward a climax, from walking to soaring, which is psychologically more satisfying.

The prophet, however, does not opt for psychological lift. He opts for realism. The hardest challenges in life come, not at the point of our soaring or of our running, but at the point of our weakness and helplessness, in times when we find it hard to keep going. And there are more of those times in the Christian's life than there are times of soaring and running. In times when there is no occasion to soar and no place to run, the promise of strength to walk and not faint, minor though it may seem, becomes of major importance. And we may eventually discover that it is the greatest of the three—as did Samuel Schereschewsky.

Samuel Schereschewsky was a rabbinical student in Russian Lithuania. One day he came into the possession of a Hebrew translation of the New Testament. Reading it, he began to entertain the possibility that Jesus was the Messiah of his people after all.

His spiritual quest led him to Germany and in 1854 to New York City where he became a Christian the following year. He eventually prepared for the priesthood in the Episcopal church. Influenced by one of the first missionaries to China, Schereschewsky decided to go to China and use his exceptional linguistic talents to translate the Scriptures into Chinese. This he did, off and on, until he suffered sunstroke and became almost completely paralyzed, except for the middle finger on his right hand.

Forced to return to America, Schereschewsky immediately set to work to complete his work of translation. As no Chinese scholar was available to serve as scribe, and as he was unable to write himself, he poked out on a typewriter with his one finger the English equivalents of the Chinese characters. When his one active finger would grow tired, he would stomp out the letters with a small stick clutched in his fist.

He produced two translations, one in Mandarin for the common people and one in Easy Wenli for the educated. He then set sail with his manuscripts to China where, with the help of Chinese assistants, he published the manuscripts and then proceeded to prepare reference Bibles in each of the dialects.

Schereschewsky died one week after he finished his work—a fulfillment of his prayer: "I am never without pain . . . when I have done this book I pray the dear Lord to take me to himself."

Schereschewsky's story is like John Claypool's. Both stories bear witness that God gives strength to walk and not faint, just enough power not to give up.

Very well, you say. This takes care of John Claypool. But what about his daughter Laura Lue? Was God's power also in her? God may have been faithful to his promise and given John Claypool strength to walk, but where was his power when Laura Lue was hurting so intensely? Where was it when she finally stopped breathing?

Claypool has no answer to this question. The road called "total understanding," he writes, holds "no promise of leading out of the darkness where I lost my child."

But Claypool does have a reply. And his reply is the insight that life is a gift. And learning to apply this insight to his daughter's life and death is one of the greatest challenges he ever faced.

The story in which Abraham is told to offer his son Isaac as a sacrifice helped Claypool to understand his own sacrifice more deeply. Earlier in his life, the whole episode of Abraham and Isaac used to bother him. What kind of God, he wondered, demands a person's child as proof of devotion? As he moved deeper into the story, however, he came to realize that the point at issue was not that at all. "What God was trying to teach Abraham here and throughout his whole existence was the basic understanding that life is gift—pure, simple, sheer gift—and that we here on earth are to relate to it accordingly." Life is a gift, and it is to be received and handled with gratitude.

This insight does not necessarily make things easy. But at least it makes things bearable when we ask questions like: "Why are children of promise cut down at the age of ten?"

In his book *Opening Blind Eyes*, John Claypool asks: "Who was Laura Lue, really?" His answer: "She had been a gift—not something I had created and therefore had the right to clutch as an owned possession, but a treasure who had always belonged to Another. She had been with me solely through the gracious generosity of that One."

The perception of life as possession and that of life as gift lead to different lifestyles. When we view life as our rightful possession, we easily lapse into remorse at the death of our child. When we view life as a gift we focus on the wonder that this child was given to us at all. Then we can learn to be grateful that our lives joined, even for a short couple of years.

There is great potency in the vision of life as gift. Such a vision leads to gratitude, and the way of gratitude "somehow puts some light around the darkness and builds strength to begin to move on." Though we may walk with a limp, like Jacob, we move on.

God's power came to John Claypool at the point of his greatest weakness, bringing light to his eyes to see life as gift and giving him strength to walk and not faint.

Coming back to our earlier question, we ask again: "But where in Laura Lue's sickness and death was God's power at work?" Claypool's answer is: In the transformation of one kind of life into another.

Why do we fear death? Because it robs us of what we think rightfully belongs to us. Death mocks all our pretensions at being the possessor of life. No one who lives can evade death for long. Death steals everything. It turns to dust everything it touches. This the Christian faith concedes, and this is why the Christian faith makes death its central problem.

Death, says faith, does not annihilate, does not steal. Death essentially transforms. This is true on the material level. You cannot destroy matter. If you try, it changes forms on you. What happens when you burn a log? Does it go out of existence? No! It transforms into smoke and ashes. And these new forms under which the log now appears are immediately caught back up in the cycles and processes of nature. Nothing is lost, for matter is indestructible.

What holds true for matter also holds true for people. Our life is but a series of transformations. We die to one form and are born to another. When we were six years old we thought our world was coming to an end when we were told we had to go to school. In a real sense, it was. But through the death of our pre-school world a new world that we didn't even know existed began to open up for us. We let go of smaller things and received bigger things in their place.

At the end of our life, Claypool says in a 1978 *Wittenburg Door* interview, "there's going to be a similar kind of transition experience. And if we can get at the terror of death by saying it is a transformer rather than an annihilator, then also we can rid the idea that death is a thief and is taking something that is rightfully ours, which is the basis of all the rage that I know—'Why did God take this—He had no right?'"

The reason God so often appears to be weak is because his power is at work precisely where we don't anticipate it to be—in our weakness and our dying, rather than in our strength and in our living. Never is God's power limited so that it cannot ultimately redeem our situation, as Harold Kushner wants us to believe in his book *When Bad Things Happen to Good People*.

Harold Kushner

Harold Kushner, like Don Wanderhope and John Claypool, went through the anguish and agony of losing a child. Like them, he took with him into the valley of suffering a vision of God—that of a God who not only appears weak but actually is weak.

At the age of eight months his son Aaron stopped gaining weight. After his first birthday his hair started falling out. At age three his condition was finally diagnosed as *progeria*, "rapid aging." This meant that Aaron would look like a little old man while still a child and that he would die while still in his teens.

Like most of his readers, Kushner had grown up with an image of God as an all-powerful, all-wise, and benevolent parent who treats us like a good earthly parent does, only better. If we obey him, he blesses us. If we disobey him, he disciplines us. He protects us from harm and danger and makes sure that we get what we deserve. Like most people, Kushner was not acquainted with deep pain. He was unfamiliar with unfair, unnecessary, and undeserved pain caused by tragic accidents, crippling diseases, and mental retardation.

The doctor's explanation of the word *progeria* plunged him in a crisis of faith. "This is not how the world is supposed to work. This can't be happening. Not to my son, not to me, if what I believe about God is true."

In his despair Kushner turned to religious literature

for answers and comfort, only to be deeply disappointed. For what he mostly found were pious attempts at defending God's good reputation. Among them were these:

1. God gives us what we deserve. What we suffer are the wages of our sins. God's world is a tit-for-tat world. Each sin is balanced off with a punishment. Perhaps not right away, but certainly in due course.

2. God must have his reasons for doing this. It's not for us to question him. Everything that happens, happens for a reason. Our life is like a beautiful tapestry. What we see of it now is the bottom side, the side with the hodgepodge of threads all going off in different directions. But you just wait. One day God will show us that the finished pattern is a work of art into which our sufferings fit beautifully.

3. God is teaching us a lesson. By sending suffering God may be telling us that he doesn't want us to be rich or successful or in love or drunk. Through a retarded child he may be teaching us patience and compassion.

4. God is testing us. He never sends burdens too heavy for us to carry. He has us go through ordeals to test the strength of our faith. When we pass the test, he will reward us.

5. God wishes to lead us to a better place. He sends suffering to liberate us from a world of sin and pain and bring us to a place where death and mourning and crying and pain shall be no more, where those who died prematurely will be reunited with the ones they loved.

All these "answers" to the problem of deep pain have one thing in common. All assume that God is the author of it. All claim to answer the question of *why* God wants us to suffer. All assert that the pain we suffer issues from the will of God.

This Kushner refuses to believe. "Bad things do happen to good people in this world, but it is not God who wills it." Not God but chaos causes us to suffer deep pain. God tamed but did not conquer chaos. Creation is the long process of replacing chaos with order. It still continues. "The world is mostly an orderly, predictable place, showing ample evidence of God's thoroughness and handiwork, but pockets of chaos remain." And as long as these pockets of chaos remain, tragedy and suffering will continue to happen, not as issues of God's will but as forays from the dark and formless world that as yet has not yielded to God's creative order.

Kushner believes that God is all-loving. But he does not believe God is all-powerful. The bad things that happen are simply beyond his control. He wills our good but cannot always give it. He is not responsible for the bad things that happen to us. These come to us from a realm God does not control. God, you might say, is an impotent fellow-sufferer, as helpless in the face of evil as we are. The best he can do is suffer with us. Were he all-powerful, he would have created a world from which pain and suffering are absent.

Is Kushner right about the will of God? Do pain and suffering happen for some reason other than the will of God? Do they happen in spite of the will of God? Do they happen because God is not powerful enough to prevent them?

The Will of God

Kushner talks about "the will of God." But he does so rather loosely. This looseness creates much confusion. To speak more meaningfully about the will of God we must make a few distinctions. We must introduce the kind of distinctions Leslie Weatherhead makes in his booklet *The*

Will of God. The difficult subject of the will of God, Weatherhead claims, demands that we introduce this threefold division:

1. The intentional will of God

2. The circumstantial will of God

3. The ultimate will of God

As long as we use the phrase "the will of God" to cover all three, without making any distinction between them, we run into the kind of trouble Kushner runs into. We then reduce God to the kind of God who, because of evil circumstances, is kept from ultimately realizing his original intentions. We then reduce God to a salvager who makes the best out of a bad situation.

To make this concrete, let us look at the story of Joseph in the Book of Genesis.

What is the intentional will of God for Joseph? Is it that Joseph shall be hated by his brothers and sold by them into slavery? Obviously not. God's intention, rather, is that Joseph and his brothers shall get along, that peace shall prevail among them. "How good and pleasant it is when brothers live together in unity! . . . For there the Lord bestows his blessing" (Psalm 133).

God's intention, however, is frustrated by certain circumstances. Joseph's lack of good judgment and his brothers' jealousy create a set of evil circumstances that cuts across God's original intention. As a result, the peace of Jacob's family is destroyed, Joseph is sold into slavery, and the brothers deceive their father.

Are all these things the intentional will of God? Obviously not. Still, they do not keep God from carrying out what he originally intended. Through the evil circumstances God carries forward his plan for Joseph and the brothers. In the very midst of them God is with Joseph and causes all he does to prosper in his hands. Given such circumstances, it is God's circumstantial will that Joseph be sold to Potiphar, be tempted by Potiphar's wife, land in prison, meet Pharaoh's cupbearer, and be introduced to the Egyptian court.

God also has an ultimate will. In spite of the brothers' hatred and Joseph's lack of discretion, God, in and through the bad things that happen, arrives at the same goal he would have arrived at had his intentional will not been frustrated. That's why, at the end of the story, Joseph and his brothers are reconciled. Once more, peace prevails in Jacob's family.

Many things in life are not God's will in the sense that they are not his intention. That sixty-six million Russians perished in the Gulag Archipelago and six million Jews in the Holocaust, these and many other things are not the intentional will of God.

Our free will, however, creates evil circumstances that cut across God's intentions so that for the time being they cannot reach their intended goal. It is during this temporary setback of God's intentional will that his circumstantial will becomes operative.

The deaths of Carol Wanderhope and Laura Lue Claypool and Aaron Kushner were not God's intentional will. God's intentional will for them was that they be healthy and live a full life.

When, however, they became terminally ill, there was a will of God even within their disease. God's power was not frustrated simply because it could not realize God's original intentions for these children.

A European colleague of mine contracted cancer and in his bout against this killer disease reached the point where he could no longer believe what one of the confessions of his denomination teaches, that the almighty and ever present power of God upholds heaven and earth and all creatures, and so rules them that rain and drought, fruitful and lean year, health and sickness— all things, in fact, come to us not by chance but from his fatherly hand.

"I can no longer believe this," he wrote. "I cannot believe that my cancer comes to me from God's fatherly hand."

Nor can I believe such a thing—if for no other reason than that it is in conflict with what Paul says in 1 Thessalonians 5:18: "Give thanks in all circumstances."

We must give thanks *in* all circumstances, not *for* all circumstances. The difference in prepositions is crucial. We must give thanks *for* rain but *in* drought, *for* fruitful years but *in* lean years, *for* health but *in* sickness.

Health and sickness do not come to us in the same way. Our health is something God originally intended. Our sickness is not. Still, this does not keep God from achieving what he originally intended.

How are we to think of God's ultimate will? Picture, says Weatherhead, a stream running down the side of a mountain to join a river in the valley below. If we wish, we can divert that stream by building a dam in its path. But no matter how hard we try, we never prevent the stream from reaching the river down below.

The ultimate will of God is like that mountain stream. No matter what obstacles block its path, nothing can prevent it from reaching its final goal.

It is wrong, therefore, to say, that nothing can happen unless it is the will of God. Lots of things can happen that are not his intentional will. It's better to say that nothing can happen that will defeat God's original intention.

Because so many people seek happiness, William Willimon writes in his book *Sighing for Eden*, they are always shocked by the arrival of deep pain as if it were somehow terribly unfair. "But the Christian was never encouraged to seek happiness in itself. We were never promised a rose garden. We were only promised that, in the end, we should have communion with the One who created us, loved us, suffered with us and for us, so that he might always have and enjoy us."

This promise in the ultimate victory of God's intentions enables us to live with many unanswered questions. We may not know now, but we believe that God is working his purpose out through the bad things that happen to us. God is not a salvaging God. He does not salvage what he can from our bad situations. God, rather, is a saving God whose power, often disguised as weakness and often operating within our weaknesses, enables him to achieve the things he originally intended.

Pain, disease, death—all these and many other bad things can make us feel miserable, cut us down, destroy our happiness, and take our lives.

But one thing they cannot do. They cannot frustrate God's intentional will for us. They cannot come between us and the love of God made flesh in Jesus Christ. God's almighty power will see to it that they won't.

Bibliography

The author acknowledges varying degrees of indebtedness to the following works, most of which were quoted or described in the text of this book:

Bailey, Kenneth E. *Through Peasant Eyes*. Grand Rapids: Eerdmans, 1980.

Boorstin, Daniel J. *The Image*. New York: Atheneum, 1961.

Brown, Robert M. "Two Marys, Two Gospels." *Christianity and Crisis* (October 3, 1977).

_____. *Elie Wiesel: Messenger to All Humanity*. Notre Dame, Indiana: University of Notre Dame Press, 1983.

Brueggemann, Walter. *The Land*. Philadelphia: Fortress Press, 1977.

Buber, Martin. *On Judaism*. Edited by Nahum N. Glatzer. New York: Schocken, 1967.

Buechner, Frederick. *Telling the Truth: The Gospel as Tragedy, Comedy, and Fairy Tale*. San Francisco: Harper & Row, 1977.

Cailliet, Emile. *Journey into Light*. Grand Rapids: Zondervan, 1968.

Chichester, Francis. *Alone Over the Tasman Sea*. London: Allen & Unwin, 1945.

Claypool, John. *Tracks of a Fellow Struggler*. Waco, Texas: Word, 1974.

_____. *Opening Blind Eyes*. Nashville: Abingdon, 1983.

Cohn, Norman. *The Pursuit of the Millennium*. Revised. New York: Oxford University Press, 1970.

De Unamuno, Miguel. *Abel Sanchez and Other Stories*. Chicago: Regnery, 1956.

De Vries, Peter. *The Blood of the Lamb*. Boston: Little, Brown, 1962.

Dostoyevski, Fyodor. *Crime and Punishment.* New York: Random House, 1959.

Endo, Shusaku. *Silence.* New York: Taplinger, 1980. First published in 1969.

Ericson, Edward E., Jr. *Solzhenitsyn: The Moral Vision.* Grand Rapids: Eerdmans, 1980.

Falwell, Jerry. *Listen, America!* New York: Doubleday, 1980.

Fortmann, Han. *Discovery of the East: Reflections on a New Culture.* Notre Dame, Indiana: Fides, 1971.

Frankl, Viktor E. *Man's Search for Meaning.* New York: Pocket Books, 1959.

Gardner, Martin. *The Flight of Peter Fromm.* Los Altos, California: Kaufmann, 1973.

Glatzer, Nahum N. *Franz Kafka: The Complete Stories.* New York: Schocken, 1971.

Greene, Graham. *The Power and the Glory.* New York: Time, 1962. First published 1940.

Hilberg, Raul. *The Destruction of the European Jews.* New York: Holmes & Meier, 1985.

Hitler, Adolf. *Mein Kampf.* New York: Reynal & Hitchcock, 1939.

Küng, Hans. *On Being Christian.* New York: Doubleday, 1976.

Kushner, Harold S. *When Bad Things Happen to Good People.* New York: Schocken, 1981.

Lindsey, Hal. *The 1980s: Countdown to Armageddon.* New York: Bantam, 1980.

McFague TeSelle, Sallie. *Speaking in Parables.* Philadelphia: Fortress, 1975.

McLoughlin, William G. *Billy Graham: Revivalist in a Secular Age.* New York: Ronald Press, 1960.

Munk, Kaj. *Troost en Tucht.* (Dutch translation of Munk's first and last sermons.) The Hague: Daamen, 1948.

_____. *Five Plays.* Translated from the Danish by R. P. Keigwin. New York: The American-Scandinavian Foundation, 1953.

Nehru, Jawaharlal. *Jawaharlal Nehru: An Autobiography.* London: The Bodley Head, 1953.

Oden Thomas C., ed. *Parables of Kierkegaard.* Princeton, New Jersey: Princeton University Press, 1978.

Ruether, Rosemary Radford. *Faith and Fratricide: The Theological Roots of Anti-Semitism.* New York: Seabury Press, 1974.

Schweizer, Eduard. *Luke: A Challenge to Present Theology.* Atlanta: John Knox, 1982.

Sittler, Joseph. *Gravity and Grace.* Minneapolis: Augsburg, 1986.

Solzhenitsyn, Aleksandr. *One Day in the Life of Ivan Denisovich.* New York: Bantam, 1963.

Tanakh: A New Translation of the Holy Scriptures According to the Traditional Hebrew Text. Philadelphia, New York, Jerusalem: The Jewish Publication Society, 1985.

Tolstoi, Leo. *The Works of Leo Tolstoi.* New York: Walter J. Black, 1928.

Wallis, Jim. "Recovering the Evangel." *Theology Today* (July 1981).

Weatherhead, Leslie D. *The Will of God.* Nashville: Abingdon, 1972.

Wiesel, Elie. *Night.* New York: Avon, 1960.

_____. *Zalmen, or the Madness of God.* New York: Random House, 1974.

_____. "The Holocaust as Literary Inspiration." *Dimensions of the Holocaust.* Lectures at Northwestern University. Evanston, Illinois: Northwestern University, 1977.

_____. *A Jew Today.* New York: Random House (Vintage), 1978.

Willimon, William H. *Sighing for Eden: Sin, Evil and the Christian Faith.* Nashville: Abingdon, 1985.

God of Weakness
was typeset on a Mergenthaler Linotron 202/N.
The text is set in 11 point Palatino,
originally designed by Hermann Zapf,
and chosen for its freshness
and slightly calligraphic feel.
Compositor: Nancy Wilson
Editors: John Sloan and Bob Hudson
Printer: Color House Graphics
Grand Rapids, Michigan